Possessions and Family in the Writings of Luke

Possessions and Family in the Writings of Luke

Questioning the Unity of Luke's Ethics

Stefan Nordgaard

Museum Tusculanum Press

Possessions and Family in the Writings of Luke:
Questioning the Unity of Luke's Ethics
Stefan Nordgaard

Consultant: Mogens Müller
Copy editor: Trevor Curnow
Layout and typesetting: Erling Lynder
Cover design: Jordy Findanis
Set in Arno and printed on Lessebo Smooth Ivory 115 g
Printed in Denmark by Narayana Press, www.narayanapress.dk
ISBN 978 87 635 4494 8

MIX
Paper from responsible sources
FSC® C010651

This book is published with financial support from
VELUX FONDEN

Museum Tusculanum Press
Dantes Plads 1, 3.th
1556 Copenhagen V
Denmark
www.mtp.dk

Contents

1
Introduction

The question of the relationship between Luke and Acts has been subject to intense scholarly debate over the last couple of decades. This has not always been the case. In the mid-1920s, H. J. Cadbury defined their relationship in a way that was to command general assent for more than half a century. Biblical interpreters had always agreed, at least since the time of Irenaeus, that Luke and Acts were written by the same author. But in a series of articles from 1925 and 1926, and particularly in his famous 1927 monograph *The Making of Luke-Acts* (followed by a second edition in 1958), Cadbury suggested that the two writings were not merely by the same author, but also parts of the same work—volumes one and two of a single composition, as it were. To illustrate their interconnectedness, he coined the title "Luke-Acts," with the hyphen designating more than just authorial unity. A famous excerpt from *The Making of Luke-Acts* captures the essence of his proposition,

> The recognition of the common authorship of Luke and Acts is not enough. They are not merely two independent writings from the same pen; they are a single continuous work. Acts is neither an appendix nor an afterthought. It is probably an integral part of the author's original plan and purpose.[1]

To Cadbury, the hyphenated title seemed slightly inelegant.[2] Nonetheless, it soon caught on (as he himself noted with some pleasure in his preface to the book's second edition), and his view of the intimate connection

1 H. J. Cadbury, *The Making of Luke-Acts*, 2nd ed. (London: SPCK, 1958), 8–9.
2 Ibid., 11.

between the two writings was almost universally accepted in the following decades. Of course there were dissenting voices, but they were few.[3] Most scholars, particularly from the birth of redaction criticism onwards, regarded "the unity of Luke-Acts" as axiomatic—as an assured result of biblical criticism and a required hermeneutical point of departure for any interpretation of either of Luke's volumes.

In 1993, however, M. C. Parsons and R. I. Pervo reopened the issue with the monograph *Rethinking the Unity of Luke and Acts*. In this work, they called for a reconsideration of Cadbury's position, and particularly for a more nuanced approach to the whole concept of unity than had governed Lucan scholarship in most of the twentieth century. Thus, in connection with Luke's writings, they invited the reader to distinguish between five different types of unity: (1) authorial unity, (2) canonical unity, (3) generic unity, (4) narrative unity, and (5) theological unity. They discussed each of these in turn. They immediately accepted the notion of an authorial unity, and, after a rather lengthier exercise in analysis, that of a theological unity too. Luke and Acts were indeed written by the same person and give expression to essentially the same theological outlook, although admittedly certain minor theological discrepancies may be distinguished between the two volumes.[4] By way of contrast, they firmly rejected the concept of a canonical unity—noting that in early Christianity "Luke and Acts never stood side-by-side in any canonical list," or in any collection of biblical literature[5]—and, slightly less categorically, the concepts of a generic and a narrative unity too. In the end, they concluded that Luke's writings should be seen as separate,

3 M. Dibelius, *Studies in the Acts of the Apostles* (New York, N.Y.: Charles Scribner's Sons, 1956), 2; H. Conzelmann, *The Theology of St. Luke* (New York, N.Y.: Harper, 1960), 17; S. G. Wilson, "Lukan Eschatology," *NTS* 16, no. 4 (1970): 330–47; S. D. Moore, "Are the Gospels Unified Narratives?" in *Society of Biblical Literature 1987 Seminar Papers*, ed. K. H. Richards, SBLSP 26 (Atlanta, GA: Scholars Press, 1987), 443–58; J. Dawsey, "The Literary Unity of Luke-Acts: Questions of Style: A Task for Literary Critics," *NTS* 35, no. 1 (1989): 48–66. A. C. Clark (*The Acts of the Apostles: A Critical Edition. With Introduction and Notes on Selected Passages* [Oxford: Clarendon, 1933]) even challenged the notion of authorial unity.

4 M. C. Parsons and R. I. Pervo, *Rethinking the Unity of Luke and Acts* (Minneapolis, MN: Fortress Press, 1993), 7–8, 84–114, 116, 123–6.

5 Ibid., 8.

even if closely connected, works of literature, and that Cadbury's celebrated hyphen should therefore yield to "a far from superfluous 'and.'"[6]

Parsons and Pervo's contribution revitalized the question of the link between Luke's writings. Certainly, many interpreters have persisted in simply assuming the unity of Luke and Acts, without taking much (or even any) notice of their work, as is clear from M. F. Bird's helpful survey of "The Unity of Luke-Acts in Recent Discussion."[7] Others, however, as he demonstrates, have begun to treat the issue seriously, whether briefly or at length. Among these, some have accepted and expanded on their conclusions. Most strikingly, perhaps, A. F. Gregory and C. K. Rowe have picked up on the notion of a canonical unity and shown that in the early church, according to the surviving evidence, Luke and Acts were never read or perceived as a unity.[8] Others writing in the wake of their work have acknowledged the complexity of the issue yet continued to speak of the unity of Luke's works, but now less categorically than was customary prior to 1993. In his *New Testament Christology*, for instance, F. J. Matera classifies Luke and Acts as "two stories that have a narrative unity rooted in the person of Jesus."[9] Others still have rejected their view and advanced a variety of arguments in favour of Cadbury's position. In a direct response to Parsons and Pervo, I. H. Marshall has offered three types of evidence in support of the classic view. First, Luke's prologue, with its mention of "the things" (in the plural) "that have been accomplished among us," seems to introduce not only the story of Jesus in the gospel, but also that of his followers in Acts. Second, Luke's redaction of Mark (particularly his omission of the whole of Mk. 7) suggests that he wrote his gospel with the story of Acts already in mind. And third, the ending of the gospel, especially 24:49, explicitly points forward to the beginning of Acts (cf.

6 Ibid., 126–7; cf. 20–83, 119–23.

7 M. F. Bird, "The Unity of Luke-Acts in Recent Discussion," *JSNT* 29, no. 4 (2007): 425–48.

8 A. F. Gregory, *The Reception of Luke and Acts in the Period before Irenaeus: Looking for Luke in the Second Century*, WUNT 2.169 (Tübingen: Mohr Siebeck, 2003); C. K. Rowe, "History, Hermeneutics, and the Unity of Luke-Acts," *JSNT* 28, no. 2 (2005): 131–57.

9 F. J. Matera, *New Testament Christology* (Louisville, KY: Westminster John Knox Press, 1999), 50–1.

Acts 2:1–4).[10] To a large extent, Marshall's reasoning builds on previous research,[11] and his points have been reiterated by scholars such as J. B. Green, B. Witherington, and G. E. Sterling, some of whom have also identified passages in Acts that presume and point back to the story of the gospel.[12] Parsons and Pervo have likewise been challenged by R. C. Tannehill, who notes that Luke and Acts must be considered as a "unified narrative" since they reflect a shared "underlying purpose," namely "God's purpose in bringing salvation to all flesh,"[13] and by L. C. A. Alexander, who suggests that the beginning of the gospel and the ending of Acts provide Luke's oeuvre with a narrative framework that allows it to be decoded, retrospectively at least, as a unity.[14]

10 I. H. Marshall, "Acts and the 'Former Treatise,'" in *The Book of Acts in Its First Century Setting. Vol. 1: Ancient Literary Setting*, ed. B. W. Winter and A. D. Clarke (Grand Rapids, MI: Eerdmans, 1993), 172–7.

11 Cf. R. Maddox, *The Purpose of Luke-Acts*, FRLANT 126 (Edinburgh: T. & T. Clark, 1982), 3–6; R. Pesch, *Die Apostelgeschichte*, EKK 5 (Zürich: Benziger, 1986), 1.24–5; C. K. Barrett, "The Third Gospel as a Preface to Acts? Some Reflections," in *The Four Gospels 1992 (FS Frans Neirynck). Vol. 2*, ed. F. van Segbroeck et al., BETL 100 (Leuven: Leuven University Press, 1992), 1451–66.

12 J. B. Green, *The Gospel of Luke*, NICNT (Grand Rapids, MI: Eerdmans, 1997), 6–10; B. Witherington, *The Acts of the Apostles: A Socio-Rhetorical Commentary* (Grand Rapids, MI: Eerdmans, 1998), 4–8; G. E. Sterling, "'Opening the Scriptures': The Legitimation of the Jewish Diaspora and the Early Christian Mission," in *Jesus and the Heritage of Israel: Luke's Narrative Claim upon Israel's Legacy*, ed. D. P. Moessner, Luke the Interpreter of Israel. Vol. 1 (Harrisburg, PA: Trinity Press, 1999), 199–217.

13 R. C. Tannehill, "The Story of Israel within Luke's Narrative," in *Jesus and the Heritage of Israel: Luke's Narrative Claim upon Israel's Legacy*, ed. D. P. Moessner, Luke the Interpreter of Israel. Vol. 1 (Harrisburg, PA: Trinity Press, 1999), 339; cf. R. C. Tannehill, *The Narrative Unity of Luke-Acts: A Literary Interpretation. Vol. 1: The Gospel according to Luke* (Philadelphia, PA: Fortress Press, 1986); R. C. Tannehill, *The Narrative Unity of Luke-Acts: A Literary Interpretation. Vol. 2: The Acts of the Apostles* (Minneapolis, MN: Fortress Press, 1994).

14 L. C. A. Alexander, "Reading Luke-Acts from Back to Front," in *The Unity of Luke-Acts*, ed. J. Verheyden, BETL 142 (Leuven: Leuven University Press, 1999), 438–41. For a fuller representation of the *status quaestionis* see, e.g., the essays collected in J. Verheyden, *The Unity of Luke-Acts*, BETL 142 (Leuven: Leuven University Press, 1999) and A. F. Gregory and C. K. Rowe, *Rethinking the Unity and Reception of Luke and Acts* (Columbia, S.C.: University of South Carolina Press, 2010), the latter of which includes reprints of Bird, "Unity of Luke-Acts," and Rowe, "History, Hermeneutics, and the Unity," in addition to C. K. Rowe, "Literary Unity and Reception History Reading Luke-Acts as Luke and Acts," *JSNT* 29, no. 4 (2007): 449–57, to be cited below.

Parsons and Pervo's book did not produce agreement, and neither was it intended to. What the two authors aimed to achieve was the revival of a discussion that had long been considered unnecessary. In that they were successful. Since its publication, scholarly treatments of the connection between Luke's writings have proliferated, and a diversity of opinions has emerged. Many scholars now hold that what was previously regarded as an exegetical given must now be perceived as an object of research. And that, I believe, is a felicitous outcome, for which it deserves praise.

The present book also explores the relationship between Luke and Acts. And I would like to think of it as continuing the line of those works that have challenged their unity. It will differ from other works in that line in three respects, however. First, it will focus on two topics to which these books and articles have only devoted little if any attention. Thus, it will examine Luke's treatment of material possessions and family. For the sake of convenience, I shall occasionally refer to his treatment of these topics as his "ethics" (although I realize, of course, that properly speaking Luke's ethics involve more than his thoughts on these particular matters). Second, it will suggest that Luke's attitude to these topics developed considerably from one work to the other, from an essentially ascetic position in the gospel to a rather more (for want of a better word) "bourgeois" position in Acts. Thus, I will attempt to show that in his gospel, Luke invites his readers to regard material wealth and marriage and attachment to family members as unacceptable for Christians and incompatible with salvation through Christ, whereas in Acts he conveys quite the opposite message, namely that these are unobjectionable and not a hindrance to salvation. In contrast to this, most scholars who have previously questioned the unity of Luke and Acts have held that whatever differences we may detect between these writings, Luke's *teaching* should be seen to have remained essentially unchanged. We noted above that Parsons and Pervo broadly accept the notion of a "theological unity" between Luke and Acts. In his more recent book on the dating of Acts, Pervo expresses a similar view.[15] And in two different articles, Rowe avers that the "theological unity of Luke-Acts" cannot "be called into

15 R. I. Pervo, *Dating Acts: Between the Evangelists and the Apologists* (Santa Rosa, CA: Polebridge Press, 2006), 12.

question,"[16] and that we ought to speak of Luke-Acts, as distinct from Luke *and* Acts, "when thinking in terms of Lucan theology, Christology, politics etc."[17] Third, it will seek to explain this change in Luke's stance on these matters through reference to an individual who is rarely ascribed any significance for Luke's thinking (by either those who advocate unity or those who advocate disunity between Luke's volumes), which is to say, the "most excellent Theophilus," to whom he dedicates his works.

In the remainder of this chapter I will seek to clarify, initially, what I mean by this third point. I will do so in three steps. First, I will discuss who this Theophilus may have been. Then I will consider a few "preliminary questions," two of which concern the connection between Luke and Acts, whereas a third concerns Theophilus. And lastly, I will try to explain exactly how I believe that Theophilus may be able to help us shed light on the development in Luke's teaching, or "ethics," as summarized above. Having done this, I will proceed to consider a few introductory questions (about the date of Luke's writings, their place of origin, and the sources available to him). And finally, in the last section, I will lay out the plan of the rest of this book.

Theophilus

We shall begin by focusing on Theophilus. Who may this person have been? In the history of research, scholars have come up with various ideas.[18] Among the more prominent ones are the suggestions that

16 Rowe, "History, Hermeneutics, and the Unity," 132 n. 3.

17 Rowe, "Literary Unity and Reception," 452.

18 For a helpful overview of the history of research see C. Heil and T. Klampfl "Theophilos (Lk 1,3; Apg 1,1)," in *"Licht zur Erleuchtung der Heiden und Herrlichkeit für dein Volk Israels": Studien zum lukanischen Doppelwerk (FS Josef Zmijewski)*, ed. C. G. Müller, BBB 151 (Hamburg, 2005), 7–28. It has sometimes been suggested that Theophilus should not be taken as a real person, but rather as a symbolic reference to the implied reader of Luke's works, or simply to any Christian ("Theophilus" being translatable as either "lover of God" or "dear to God"). This proposal goes back to at least Origen (*Hom. in Lucam* 1.10–11), but is now generally rejected. Green (*Luke*, 44) sums up the major arguments against it, "(1) Theophilus is a common name, found in the papyri and inscriptions as early as the third century B.C.E.; (2) the appellation 'most excellent' would then be pointless; and (3) a symbolic dedication of this sort would be unparalleled in Luke's literary culture."

he could have been Luke's publisher[19] or a non-Christian magistrate invoked by Luke "to deal fairly with the Christians."[20] Neither of these seems convincing, however, as modern scholarship has generally come to recognize. The former clearly rests on anachronistic assumptions, since, as R. Winsbury and others have demonstrated, book production did not really involve publishers, or even publishing in our sense of the term, in the ancient world.[21] And the latter blatantly disregards significant portions of Luke's text. Luke's writings, according to this view, should be seen as a formal apology addressed to Theophilus in order to convince him of the falsity of certain rumours to which, allegedly, he should have been exposed (cf. Lk. 1:4). These rumours would have identified the members of the church as politically unruly and a threat to the public order. Yet although (as we shall see in chapter 2) Luke's writings do contain a lot of apologetic, they also contain considerable amounts of material to which a Roman administrator called upon to exonerate the Christians could only be expected to show indifference. As C. K. Barrett once put it, "No Roman official would ever have filtered out so much of what to him would be theological and ecclesiological rubbish in order to reach so tiny a grain of relevant apology."[22] Furthermore, Luke's writings seem to presume an audience considerably more at home in the world of Judaism than one could generally expect of a Roman magistrate. As S. Mason has noted, Luke consistently "mentions Sabbath, circumcision, the law, Abraham, and Moses as if their value and meaning were self-evident to the reader."[23]

In what follows, I shall not attempt to arrive at a detailed understanding of who Theophilus was. To avoid unnecessary speculation (and heeding the principle of Occam's razor), I shall aim only for as much of a shadowy outline as will be necessary to enable ourselves to make use of him to explain the differences I have outlined above and shall explore in

19 E. J. Goodspeed, "Some Greek Notes: Was Theophilus Luke's Publisher?" *JBL* 73, no. 2 (1954): 84–92.

20 H. J. Cadbury, "The Purpose Expressed in Luke's Preface," *Expositor* 21 (1921): 437.

21 R. Winsbury, *The Roman Book: Books, Publishing and Performance in Classical Rome*, Classical Literature and Society (London: Duckworth, 2009), 53–75, 95–110.

22 C. K. Barrett, *Luke the Historian in Recent Study* (London: Epworth, 1961), 63.

23 S. Mason, *Josephus and the New Testament*, 2nd ed. (Peabody, MS: Hendrickson Publishers, 2003), 266.

the rest of this book between the ethics of Luke and Acts. I shall therefore confine myself to establishing a rather rough sketch of what I perceive to have been his most likely (i) religious, (ii) ethnic, and (iii) social profiles.

(i) Religious profile. We may safely assume that Theophilus was familiar with the Christian faith prior to his reading of Luke's gospel, since in its preface Luke claims to have written that work in order to provide Theophilus with what he terms "certainty" or "certain knowledge" about the things of which he had previously "been informed" (1:4, ἵνα ἐπιγνῷς περὶ ὧν κατηχήθης λόγων τὴν ἀσφάλειαν).[24] The question of how Theophilus was familiar with Christianity is a matter of dispute, however. As indicated above, those scholars who perceived Theophilus as a non-Christian magistrate understood Luke to be alluding in the preface to the existence of malicious rumours about the church of which Theophilus should have been aware (for further references see chapter 2). Partly owing to the weaknesses connected with that view, most interpreters today, however, take him to be referring instead to some form of initial training in the Christian faith that Theophilus should have received. I find no reason to object to this view. Accordingly, like these commentators, I understand Theophilus to have been, at the time of the composition of Luke's gospel, a relatively recent convert to the church and a newly arrived member of Luke's community.[25] It has admittedly been suggested that Theophilus could also have been "a sympathetic outsider" with whom Luke and/or other members of his community had previously been in contact.[26] Yet while this remains a possibility, I find it less easy to imagine that Luke should have chosen to dedicate his work to an open-minded outsider rather than to a person already enrolled in

24 Translations are my own unless otherwise indicated. Often, however, my renderings of biblical texts do not deviate much, if at all, from the NRSV, which I have consulted throughout.

25 E.g., I. H. Marshall, *The Gospel of Luke: A Commentary on the Greek Text*, NIGTC (Exeter: Paternoster, 1978), 43; J. A. Fitzmyer, *The Gospel According to Luke (I–IX): Introduction, Translation, and Notes*, AB 28 (Garden City, N.Y.: Doubleday, 1981), 299–300; L. T. Johnson, *The Gospel of Luke*, SP 3 (Collegeville, MI: Liturgical Press, 1991), 28; Witherington, *Acts*, 63–65.

26 C. F. Evans, *Saint Luke*, TPINTC (London; Philadelphia: SCM Press, 1990), 135–6; Green, *Luke*, 44–45; L. C. A. Alexander, "What If Luke Had Never Met Theophilus?" *BibInt* 8, no. 1 (2000): 161–70.

the fellowship of belief. Furthermore, as B. Witherington notes, Luke would hardly have paraphrased the subject matter of his work as "the things that have been fulfilled among us (ἐν ἡμῖν)" (Lk. 1:1), unless he had somehow conceived of Theophilus as an insider.[27]

(ii) Ethnic profile. A number of interpreters believe that Theophilus was a Jew. Some of these take him to have been a member of Luke's community—someone who had come to Christianity "from a synagogue setting";[28] others perceive him as an outsider.[29] The name Theophilus was common in the ancient Mediterranean and used by both Jews and gentiles.[30] Nothing in Luke's prefaces allows us to determine the ethnicity of Theophilus with any kind of certainty. As will emerge from chapter 2, however, I find it exceedingly unlikely that Luke's community should have comprised any members of a Jewish origin—like E. Haenchen, I believe that Acts 28:25–28, among several other passages, clearly communicates that Luke had "written the Jews off"[31] and that he perceived the Christian community as an exclusively gentile affair, no longer open to Jewish conversions. Yet as I have already noted, I do believe that Theophilus was a member of the Christian community. The combination of these factors leads me to assume that he must have been a gentile.

(iii) Social profile. Several scholars hold that Theophilus was most likely a man of superior social status. I share that assessment. Three factors point in that direction. (a) Luke addresses him by the title κράτιστος ("most excellent"). In certain historical eras, this term was used specifically of officeholders of equestrian rank, although admittedly in the late first and early second centuries CE it had a wider

27 Witherington, *Acts*, 63.

28 E.g., ibid., 64.

29 E.g., Alexander, "What If Luke?"

30 H. J. Cadbury, "Commentary on the Preface of Luke," in *The Beginnings of Christianity. Part I: The Acts of the Apostles. Vol. II*, ed. F. Jackson and K. Lake (London: MacMillan, 1922), 138 n. 10; L. C. A. Alexander, *The Preface to Luke's Gospel: Literary Convention and Social Context in Lk. 1.1–4 and Acts 1.1*, SNTSMS 78 (Cambridge: Cambridge University Press, 1993), 133; Heil and Klampfl, "Theophilos," 16–27; M. Wolter, *Das Lukasevangelium*, HNT 5 (Tübingen: Mohr Siebeck, 2008), 66.

31 E. Haenchen, "The Book of Acts as Source Material for the History of Early Christianity," in *Studies in Luke-Acts (FS Paul Schubert)*, ed. L. E. Keck and J. L. Martyn (London: SPCK, 1968), 278.

application.[32] It is interesting to note, however, that elsewhere in his work Luke uses the title exclusively of officeholding knights (Felix: Acts 23:26; 24:2; Festus: Acts 26:25). This hardly requires us to conclude that Theophilus must have held such rank, but it certainly implies that he did belong, possibly in a less narrow sense, to the higher echelons of society.

(b) The fact that Luke dedicates his works to Theophilus suggests that Theophilus was his patron. L. C. A. Alexander admittedly cautions against this conclusion, noting that dedicatees in the ancient world were not always patrons of the authors. Sometimes they were pupils, colleagues, or family members.[33] Alexander's observation is correct, of course. But in the particular case of Luke and Theophilus, I believe that a patron-client relationship remains probable. Certainly, nothing suggests that the former was a colleague of Luke, or—even less likely—a relative (Luke's discourse on the family institution in his gospel would rather seem to preclude this, as will be clear from chapter 4). Luke may have thought of him as a pupil, but if so it is difficult to understand why he should have chosen to single this particular pupil out to be honoured in his prefaces (rather than, for instance, the whole body of neophyte Christians), unless he was also somehow his patron—which I will accordingly take him to have been. Theophilus may have been Luke's personal patron, but the more likely scenario is that he served as a patron for his community as a whole, and that he had assumed this role in connection with, or shortly after, his adoption of the Christian faith.

(c) Throughout his work, Luke exhibits a keen interest in people of wealth and in how such people may obtain salvation. I will analyse this topic in depth in chapter 3. For now it is enough to notice that this interest appears to be most easily explained if we assume that his community comprised at least one person (but possibly more) who belonged to the privileged classes. S. Légasse has identified one passage in particular that points in this direction.[34] In Luke 18:18–30 we hear of Jesus'

32 Cf. Cadbury, "Commentary on the Preface," 505–7; Alexander, *Preface to Luke's Gospel*, 132–3, 188–90.

33 Ibid., 188–91.

34 S. Légasse, *L'appel du riche (Marc 10:17–31 et parallèles): Contribution à l'étude des fondements scripturaires de l'état religieux* (Paris: Beauchesne, 1966), 97–110.

encounter with the rich ruler who wished to learn what it would take for him to inherit eternal life. The story builds on and closely mirrors that of Jesus' meeting with the rich man in Mark 10:17–31 and the rich young man in Matthew 19:16–30. Thus, like Mark and Matthew, Luke explains that Jesus charged this individual to sell all of his possessions and distribute the proceeds among the poor. Yet unlike his predecessors, Luke does not say that this person left Jesus and the disciples when their conversation had ended (cf. Mk 10:22; Mt. 19:22). He notes only that once he had received Jesus' message, "he became deeply sad; for he was very rich" (18:23). As Ph. F. Esler has put it, "the effect of this change ... is that the rich man and his problem are presented by Luke as being within the Christian community."[35] If there were rich people within Luke's community, it seems reasonable to assume that this group would have included Theophilus (if indeed he was not the only one).

Together, these three factors make it exceedingly likely that Theophilus was a person of high social standing. Exactly how high is difficult to determine. Unlike Alexander, I would not exclude the possibility that he could have been an aristocrat. Alexander dismisses this on the grounds that all of Luke's heroes are manual labourers and that "such heroes could never be taken seriously by ... aristocratic readers."[36] Her argument fails to convince, however, as we have reason to believe that several early Christians belonged to at least the lower rungs of the aristocracy, despite the fact that Jesus and his followers were nearly always perceived in the ancient world (as in the modern) as manual workers. In 1 Corinthians 1:26 Paul observes that not many of the Corinthians were powerful (δυνατοί) and noble (εὐγενεῖς) at the moment of their calling, thereby also implying that some of them were (cf. also Rom. 16:26 on Erastus). In *On Idolatry* Tertullian cites and criticizes a group of believers who held that their affluence and family backgrounds required them to take on the task of political office

35 Ph. F. Esler, *Community and Gospel in Luke-Acts: The Social and Political Motivations of Lucan Theology*, SNTSMS 57 (Cambridge: Cambridge University Press, 1987), 185; cf. Légasse, *L'appel du riche*, 97–110; R. J. Karris, "Rich and Poor: The Lukan Sitz-Im-Leben," in *Perspectives on Luke-Acts*, ed. C. H. Talbert, SSS 5 (Danville, VA: Assoc. of Baptist Professors of Religion, 1978), 123; K.-J. Kim, *Stewardship and Almsgiving in Luke's Theology*, JSNTsup 155 (Sheffield: JSOT Press, 1998), 192.

36 Alexander, *Preface to Luke's Gospel*, 177–8.

(18). And Cyprian and Gregory Thaumaturgus may have belonged to the lower *ordines*, although clearly their exact social position remains difficult to assess.[37] On the other hand, of course, nothing compels us to identify Theophilus as an aristocrat. Luke's use of the term κράτιστος could imply equestrian rank, and the somewhat curious transformation of the "rich (young) man" in Mark and Matthew into a "rich ruler" in Luke might suggest that Theophilus had held office at the time of the composition of Luke's gospel, if indeed, as Esler put it, Luke was attempting to portray "the rich man and his problem ... as being within the Christian community." Clearly, we should not push the evidence too far, and fortunately, for our present purposes we do not need to. Knowledge of Theophilus' exact social position is immaterial to the theory that I shall propose. It is enough to place him somewhere in the upper levels of society.

To summarize what has been said, we may say that at the time of the composition of Luke's gospel, Theophilus was presumably a socially advanced gentile who had recently converted to the Christian faith, and at that moment, or shortly thereafter, assumed a patron-like role in relation to Luke's community.

Preliminary Questions

Before we turn to consider how the person of Theophilus may be of service to us in explaining the properties of Luke's texts, we will need to briefly discuss three preliminary questions. As noted, the first and second of these concern the relationship between Luke and Acts, whereas the third relates to Theophilus. The questions are these. (i) Did Luke know at the time he was composing his gospel that he would later produce a sequel? (ii) How long a time elapsed between the writing of his two books? (iii) Did Theophilus read Luke's work (or, alternatively, did he have them read to him), and did Luke expect him to?

Our answer to the first question should almost certainly be in the affirmative. We noted above that scholars like Maddox, Pesch, Barrett,

37 See further L. W. Countryman, *The Rich Christian in the Church of the Early Empire: Contradictions and Accommodations*, Texts and Studies in Religion 7 (New York, N.Y.: Edwin Mellen Press, 1980).

and Marshall have pointed to a number of features in Luke's gospel that seem to indicate this. Clearly, not all of their observations are equally compelling, but I would at least agree with them that Luke's decision to omit all of Mark 7 (in a gospel that otherwise places considerable emphasis on the gentile mission; see e.g., 2:32; 4:24–27; 13:29–30) and the prediction in 24:49 are hard to explain unless we assume that he was already planning for a second volume at the time he was writing the first one. However, at the same time I would urge that nothing forces us to assume that once he actually got around to composing that second volume it turned out, in all respects, exactly as he had originally imagined or intended.

The second question is considerably harder to answer. The truth of the matter is that we have no way of knowing. However, since the two texts were apparently never read together as a unified narrative in the earliest church and never travelled together side by side in the manuscript tradition (as Gregory and Rowe have shown), it seems fair to assume that *some* time would have passed between the writing of the gospel and the writing of Acts. But whether we are talking months or years is impossible to say.[38]

Concerning the third question, the answer to both parts is quite definitely yes. It is true, of course, as scholars have sometimes noted that "literary patrons" (i.e., patrons of authors) in the ancient world often did not read the works of the authors they supported, and that those authors often did not expect them to (cf., e.g., Plin. *NH* pref. 6, written to the emperor Titus).[39] Yet Theophilus can hardly be characterized as any ordinary literary patron. Normally, when members of the upper classes became literary patrons, they did so in order to enhance their own standing in the community. Achieving this would generally not require them to read the works of their protégés. Usually, it would be quite sufficient to simply provide their protégés with various forms of backing: financial

38 It has occasionally been suggested that Acts was written before Luke; cf., e.g., H. G. Russell, "Which Was Written First, Luke or Acts?" *HTR* 48, no. 3 (1955): 167–74. This proposal, however, produces more problems than it solves. For instance, it requires that Luke's prefaces be regarded as later additions.

39 Cadbury, *Making of Luke-Acts*, 194–209; Esler, *Community and Gospel*, 24; Alexander, *Preface to Luke's Gospel*, 56–63; cf. B. K. Gold, *Literary Patronage in Greece and Rome* (Chapel Hill, N.C.; London: University of North Carolina Press, 1987).

support, access to networks, the organization of *recitationes* (semi-public readings of portions of their writings), and so on. But it seems quite obvious that Theophilus had not decided to patronize Luke (and his community) in order to boost his own social esteem. Surely, if that had been his goal, he would have been better served supporting an author who did not disseminate beliefs for which one could easily get oneself executed, and certainly publicly ridiculed, as he himself must obviously have realized. Rather, if the profile I have sketched above is correct, he had decided to do this because he had come to embrace the Christian faith and attach himself to the Christian movement. Any notion that he should have done this and then not been interested in reading or listening to Luke's works strikes me as implausible (as I believe it would have done Luke) as these works would be focusing on the beliefs and hopes that Theophilus himself had just adopted and on the history of the movement in which he himself had just enlisted. If works with such a focus did not interest him, one wonders why he would have joined the Christian movement in the first place.[40]

Luke and Theophilus

With these considerations behind us, I am now in a position to clarify how I believe Theophilus may be able to help us understand the development of Luke's ethics. To do this, I would like to propose an historical scenario for the genesis of Luke's works. This scenario will depend and slightly expand on the conclusions I have drawn above. It will be theoretical, of course, and ultimately impossible to prove. However, I hope to be able to show in this section and the rest of this book that it will at least be historically plausible and consistent with Luke's text.

Let us begin from the gospel. Luke may have had several purposes in writing his first volume. I would suggest, however, that at least one of these was to strengthen Theophilus' commitment to the church, while at the same time persuading him to change how he lived his life in quite a radical way. Let me elaborate. In chapter 2 I shall analyse Luke's

40 I recognize, of course, that this argument will have force only for those who accept that Theophilus was in fact an insider.

discourse on three different topics: Christianity and Rome, Christianity and novelty, and Christianity and the Jews. I shall attempt to show that Luke's treatment of these topics echoes traditional Roman upper class ideology and contributes to recasting the history of early Christianity in a way that could well be expected to appeal to people in socially advanced positions. Luke's approach to these themes may reveal nothing but his own personal beliefs and proclivities, but I propose to understand them as at least also reflecting a desire on his part to make Christianity seem more attractive to Theophilus, and by so doing intensify his wish to continue as a member of the Christian movement. However, Luke was not merely out to please Theophilus and make him feel more "at home" in the church. He was also attempting to make this recent convert understand that for him to remain a member of the Christian movement (if that at least was to have any soteriological effect on his part) would require him to adopt a lifestyle that differed significantly from the one he was used to. If, as I have suggested, Theophilus did belong to the comfortable classes, it is clear that he must have possessed a considerable amount of money and that he would have needed to place quite a strong emphasis on family allegiances (I will elaborate on the last of these claims at the appropriate place in chapter 4). Yet as I have noted and shall seek to demonstrate in detail in chapters 3 and 4, Luke's gospel forcefully indicates that all this is wholly incompatible with life as a Christian and the attainment of salvation. Luke's gospel will thus have conveyed to Theophilus that if his conversion was to have any beneficial effect on his part, he would need to follow it up by renouncing his social position.

Let us turn now to Acts. As noted, this second volume offers an ethical vision that differs markedly from the one we meet in the gospel. In this work, Luke signals that monetary wealth and family life are quite compatible with life as a Christian and not at all an impediment to salvation. Why did this change occur? In his monograph *The Rich Christian in the Church of the Early Empire*, L. W. Countryman demonstrates that in the early centuries, socially advanced Christians frequently failed to submit to the authority of their church officials (see, e.g., Herm. *Sim.* 8.9; *1 Clem.* 3.1–3; Cypr. *Unit.* 26).[41] This happened not least when the latter urged

41 Countryman, *Rich Christian in the Church*, 149–200.

them to wholly or partly renounce their social prerogatives as part of their Christian commitment. Several believers from prosperous backgrounds, we may then conclude, wished and insisted on their right to combine faith in Jesus and membership of the church with a socially privileged lifestyle. It is easy to imagine that Theophilus, too, could have nurtured such a wish and would have been ready to assert his right to fulfil it. I therefore propose that the most likely explanation for the change we perceive in Luke's ethics is that once his gospel was in circulation, Theophilus had reacted strongly against it and refused to submit to its imperatives, and had in the period that followed induced him to complete its sequel in a way that would authorize rather than condemn the type of existence that he had so far enjoyed. It is difficult to say just how Theophilus did this. He may have availed himself of some reasoned theological arguments, or he may have rather more bluntly exercised his influence as patron. Whatever he did, the author who had previously challenged him to renounce his social position now produced a narrative that sanctioned a form of conduct that enabled him to preserve it. We should add to this that although we perceive a significant development in Luke's ethics, nothing in his stance on the three topics mentioned above—Christianity and Rome, Christianity and novelty, and Christianity and the Jews—changed from the gospel to the Acts. His view of these issues remained constant, as we shall see in the following chapter. This, of course, is unsurprising given that nothing in Luke's discourse on these matters is likely to have dismayed Theophilus. On the contrary.

This, in brief, is the theory that I wish to develop in the course of this book. I anticipate that some readers will find it too speculative for their tastes. In a recent book, for instance, C. K. Rowe has argued that since we know so little about the context of the emergence of Luke's works, we ought to practise what he terms an "interpretive asceticism" that bids us think of his audience in purely general terms, as "Christian readers of various kinds in the late first century," and refrain from speculating about his *actual* readers.[42] In response to this and to avoid misunderstandings, I would like to emphasize that there are two steps in the

42 C. K. Rowe, *World Upside Down: Reading Acts in the Graeco-Roman Age* (Oxford; New York, N.Y.: Oxford University Press, 2009), 11.

reading I propose. The first is to study Luke's ethics and to demonstrate that these developed from his first work to the second. I complete this step quite independently of any speculation about Theophilus or any other of Luke's actual readers, and thus, one might say, "hermeneutically ascetically," to adopt Rowe's terminology. I turn to theorizing about Theophilus only when, in a second step, I try to understand why Luke's ethics developed, and I do this because I believe that this is a question that cannot be resolved on purely text-internal grounds. Naturally, I could have chosen to then settle for simply noting this development and refrained from trying to explain it. Yet I have felt that doing so would be to leave the task of exegesis only half accomplished, and that it would be more fulfilling, after all, to tiptoe into the realm of historical speculation, with all the uncertainty that this involves, than to leave the question unexplored. It goes without saying that I recognize, and respect, that other interpreters may feel differently about this and may consider any historical reconstruction of the sort that I engage in as exegetically off limits. I would like to ask these readers, however, to assess my interpretation of Luke's writings at step one unaffected by any uneasiness they might feel with my proceedings at step two, because, as I have indicated, I take this first step independently of the second.

Further Introductory Questions

We are now nearly ready to delve into the actual examination of Luke's text. But before we do so and leave this chapter, we need to address a few further questions regarding the dating of Luke's works, their place of origin, and their sources. None of these questions is tremendously important to the reading that I shall propose. But since they will play a limited role, and since I will occasionally refer to my stance on at least some of them, they should be given a cursory treatment.

Date. Luke's writings are usually dated to the mid-80s, and thus, in terms of political history, to the reign of Domitian (81–96). Some interpreters opt for an earlier date with some of them even pointing to the early 60s, whereas others place them as late as the second century. The most systematic recent treatment of the topic is Pervo's *Dating Acts* from 2006, which focuses almost exclusively, however, on Luke's second volume. Pervo here dates the writing of Acts to 115, or at least to somewhere between 110 and 120. Some of Pervo's arguments are questionable, particularly those focused on Lucan theology and ecclesiology. But his case for familiarity on Luke's part (in Acts at least) with the last book of Josephus' *Antiquities* (completed in 93/94) and the collective body of Pauline letters (in circulation, presumably, from around 100) is generally persuasive.[43] On the whole, I therefore consider his dating of Acts likely, give or take a few years. As noted earlier, it is hard to determine how many years should be taken to separate the writing of the gospel from the writing of Acts, but I would presume the two to be less than a decade apart. I therefore consider a dating for both works to the early second century, and the reign of Trajan (98–117), plausible.

Place. Due to a number of geographical inaccuracies, scholars generally agree that Luke's writings cannot be given a Palestinian origin. Various other places have been suggested, with Rome, Antioch, Caesarea, and Corinth as some of the more popular candidates. In my assessment, however, Pervo has made a strong case for Ephesus.[44] He mentions two factors that point in this direction. First, Luke exhibits a high level of familiarity with the Aegean in general and Ephesus in particular. To some extent, this may be due to his acquaintance with the Pauline literature, but his knowledge clearly goes beyond what the letters convey (cf. Acts 19:9, 25, 29, and 35). In addition to the evidence amassed by Pervo, one may note, with S. M. Baugh and P. Trebilco, that our author also intriguingly speaks of Artemis in a way that betrays an awareness of the peculiarities of the local idiom. Thus, in accordance with inscriptions discovered in the city, he calls the Ephesian goddess by the feminine θεά when he also uses her name (19:27, τὸ τῆς μεγάλης θεᾶς Ἀρτέμιδος ἱερόν), but by the masculine form θεός when her name is not mentioned (19:37, τὴν θεόν).[45] Second, Luke also displays a remarkable degree of interest in Ephesus. In Acts, no fewer than "[s]eventy verses, c. 7 percent of the text,

43 Pervo, *Dating Acts*, 51–199. For dependence by Luke on Josephus see also Mason, *Josephus and the New Testament*, 251–95.

44 R. I. Pervo, *Acts: A Commentary*, Hermeneia (Minneapolis, MN: Fortress Press, 2009), 5–6.

45 S. M. Baugh, "Phraseology and the Reliability of Acts," *NTS* 36, no. 2 (1990): 290–94; P. Trebilco, *The Early Christians in Ephesus from Paul to Ignatius* (Grand Rapids, MI: Eerdmans, 2008), 105–6.

take place in or are related to the Asian metropolis" (three times as much as is true of any other location outside of Palestine). It is described as "the center of Paul's lengthiest mission (19:10)." And "Paul's address to the Ephesian presbyters" features as "a paradigm for all believers everywhere."[46] Decisive evidence cannot be obtained, but in my assessment the facts listed here make the city of Ephesus the most likely place of origin.

Source. I have already noted that I accept that Luke was familiar with both Josephus and the Pauline letters. Readers will have noticed, however, that I also speak of Matthew as one of Luke's sources. Behind my decision to do so lies an acceptance of what has variously been identified as "the Farrer," "the "Farrer-Goulder," and, rather more recently, "the Luke/Matthew hypothesis." This theory rejects the existence of Q, but differs from the so-called Griesbach-hypothesis in that, like the widely held two-source hypothesis, it insists on Marcan priority. Thus, it posits that Luke had access to Matthew and that both of these writers had access to Mark. The theory has recently been carefully and convincingly argued by M. S. Goodacre and F. Watson.[47] In addition to the arguments offered by these scholars, we may note that it gains credence over the two-source hypothesis if the dating of Luke and Acts that I have suggested is adopted. As W.-D. Köhler has shown, a date much later than the mid-80s for the gospel of Matthew is difficult to defend;[48] and it may seem unlikely that Luke should have been unfamiliar with this work, if in fact it had been around for nearly (or possibly more than) two decades when he started writing. Luke may have had access to sources besides the ones mentioned here (for instance, the so-called "Antiochene source"; cf. also the mention of his "many" predecessors in Lk. 1:1), but the argument in this book will not depend on any assumptions in that regard. I should mention, however, that at the end of chapter 2 I will propose that

46 Pervo, *Acts*, 6.

47 M. S. Goodacre, *The Case Against Q: Studies in Markan Priority and the Synoptic Problem* (Harrisburg, PA: Trinity Press International, 2002); F. Watson, *Gospel Writing: A Canonical Perspective* (Grand Rapids, MI: Eerdmans, 2013), 117–55.

48 W.-D. Köhler, *Die Rezeption des Matthäusevangeliums in der Zeit vor Irenäus*, WUNT 2.24 (Tübingen: Mohr, 1987).

Luke, and probably also his readers, had knowledge of some of the work of Seneca the Younger.

Structure of the Book

The book comprises five chapters, including this one. As already indicated, chapter 2 will analyse Luke's discourse on Christianity and Rome, Christianity and novelty, and Christianity and the Jews. The purpose of that chapter will be to show that Luke's approach to these topics may be seen to reflect a desire on his part to reshape Christianity in a way that would make membership of the Christian movement seem more attractive to Theophilus than might otherwise have been the case. It will emerge that Luke's attitude to these issues remained unchanged from the gospel to the Acts. Chapters 3 and 4 will focus on Luke's treatment of possessions and family, respectively. The aim of these chapters will be to demonstrate that Luke's teaching on these matters developed in the manner described above, and that the theory about the interactions between Luke and Theophilus that I have outlined in this chapter may serve as a plausible explanatory model. It will emerge from these chapters that there are a few passages in the gospel that deviate from the largely ascetic line that I will otherwise claim to characterize this text (above all, 14:12–14 and 19:1–10). I hope to be able to show that even these may be seen to make sense within the framework of the theory that I have sketched and shall develop of the relationship between Luke and his dedicatee. Chapter 5 will offer a conclusion to the study with a summary of its findings and a brief consideration of the way in which as a whole it may be seen to contribute to the debate about the unity of Luke and Acts.

2

Rome, Novelty, and the Jews

In this chapter we focus on Luke's treatment of three different themes, namely Christianity and Rome, Christianity and novelty, and Christianity and the Jews. My aim will be to show that Luke's approach to these topics may be seen to reflect an ambition on his part to render the church more attractive to Theophilus than it might otherwise have seemed, for instance in the works to which he alludes in the preface to his gospel (1:1–4), and by so doing confirm Theophilus in his belief that he was right to join the Christian movement. I would like to emphasize that I shall not attempt to prove that Luke must have designed his discourse on these issues with this particular purpose in mind. Clearly, one could argue (as I believe most scholars would) that it reflects nothing but his own genuine beliefs. What I wish to demonstrate is only that he *may* have done so, and so the theory about the importance of Theophilus for the shape of Luke's writings that I presented in the introduction and will further develop in chapters 3 and 4 is compatible with his treatment of these subjects. I shall discuss each of the subjects in turn.

Christianity and Rome

In chapter 1 I noted that previous scholarship has sometimes identified Theophilus as a non-Christian Roman magistrate. According to this perception, Luke intended to provide the Roman authorities with "certain knowledge" or "security" (ἀσφάλειαν) (Lk. 1:4) through his work about the political harmlessness of the Christian movement. This interpretation was first proposed by C. A. Heumann[1] and was subsequently adopted and developed by a number prominent scholars of the nineteenth and early-to-mid-twentieth centuries.[2] Today, for reasons given above, very few interpreters accept this view.[3] However, even if Theophilus has generally ceased to be regarded as a non-Christian magistrate and Luke and Acts as a formal apology to the state, most interpreters continue to discern in Luke's work a pervasive apologetic ambition to make Christianity come across in such a way that it is not perceived as subversive of the Roman political order.[4]

Of course, there are dissenting voices. P. Walaskay has suggested that rather than seeking to defend the church over against the empire, Luke was in fact offering an *apologia pro imperio* to the church.[5] R. J. Cassidy, in a complete reversal of received opinion, has proposed that Luke sought to demonstrate the politically disruptive power of Christianity.[6] And M. Wolter has claimed that the church's relationship to the state was of no real interest to Luke.[7] These views have received modest support, however, and for good reason. The dominant view appears justified, provided that we understand "political" here in a restricted sense. In contemporary academic parlance it is customary to think of politics as embracing or intersecting with all areas of public and sometimes even private life. And it would certainly be misguided to claim that

1 C. A. Heumann, "Dissertatio de Theophilo cui Lucas historiam sacram inscripsit," 1720, Chassis IV, Bibliotheca Historico-Philologico-Theologica.

2 To give but a few examples: E. Zeller, *Die Apostelgeschichte nach ihrem Inhalt und Ursprung kritisch untersucht* (Stuttgart: Mäcken, 1854); J. Weiss, *Über die Absicht und den literarischen Charakter der Apostelgeschichte* (Göttingen: Vandenhoeck & Ruprecht, 1897); Cadbury, "Purpose Expressed"; Conzelmann, *Theology of St. Luke*, 135.

3 However, see E. Heusler, *Kapitalprozesse im lukanischen Doppelwerk*, NTAbh Neue Folge 38 (Münster: Aschendorff, 2000), 259–60.

4 E.g., L. M. Wills, "The Depiction of the Jews in Acts," *JBL* 110, no. 4 (1991): 651–3; Esler, *Community and Gospel*, 201–19; Mason, *Josephus and the New Testament*, 251–95; Rowe, *World Upside Down*, 53–89.

5 P. Walaskay, *"And So We Came to Rome": The Political Perspective of St. Luke*, SNTSMS 49 (Cambridge: Cambridge University Press, 1983).

6 R. J. Cassidy, *Jesus, Politics and Society: A Study of Luke's Gospel* (Maryknoll, N.Y.: Orbis Books, 1978); R. J. Cassidy, *Society and Politics in the Acts of the Apostles* (Maryknoll, N.Y.: Orbis Books, 1987); cf. also Maddox, *Purpose of Luke-Acts*, 91–9.

7 M. Wolter, *Theologie und Ethos im frühen Christentum: Studien zu Jesus, Paulus und Lukas*, WUNT 236 (Tübingen: Mohr Siebeck, 2009), 388–401, esp. 400.

Luke had attempted to establish a sense of general congruity between the Christian and the Roman approaches to reality. Particularly in his gospel, as we shall see in chapters 3 and 4, but also in Acts,[8] Luke challenges an array of Roman values and sharply contrasts Christianity with various facets of pagan culture.[9] However, if we take "political" in the limited sense of relating to Rome's direct exertion of power and the military and administrative institutions through which it is channeled, and, in general, the civic order, the dominant view is hard to resist. In both of his works, Luke comes across as remarkably anxious to show that Christianity poses a threat neither to Roman rule nor to the peace and stability of the empire.

Luke's readers, and in particular recent converts, may not have perceived the political innocence of the church as a matter of course. Some early Christians clearly opposed Roman government in one way or another (e.g., John of Patmos), and the few surviving non-Christian sources that shed light on how "normal" Romans perceived early Christians suggest that members of the church could easily fall under suspicion of insurrectionism and other forms of disturbance of the civic order. In *Annals* 15.44, for instance, Tacitus reports that during the reign of Nero, Christians living in the capital were accused of setting the city on fire and executed in the most brutal ways. He furthermore testifies that Christians were commonly "hated for their *flagitia*" (tr. Jackson, LCL), i.e., for their "acts of disgrace" (whatever precisely these acts may be thought to have involved). And in *Letters* 10.96 the governor Pliny reports to Trajan that he had found the Christians of his province harmless, but only after having conducted a careful investigation of the movement which involved the torture of two slave girls carrying the titles of *ministrae*.

Why should the Romans sometimes conceive of Christians as trouble-makers and a danger to the state? At least three reasons may be

8 Cf., e.g., Rowe, *World Upside Down*, 17–51.

9 Hence, to speak with D. Marguerat (*The First Christian Historian: Writing the "Acts of the Apostles,"* SNTSMS 121 [Cambridge: Cambridge University Press, 2002], 82) of "inculturation" in Luke's work would be excessive.

given.[10] First, Christians were known to have pledged allegiance to a man commonly believed to have been executed by the Romans as an enemy of the state. Second, Christians often refused to participate in traditional forms of worship, including the cult of the emperor, which could be construed as a sign of political disloyalty. Third, the fact that Christians would often convene in what resembled private *collegia*, or "associations," or "societies," could in some cases presumably be enough to arouse suspicion. During Pliny's tenure in Pontus and Bithynia a fire had broken out in the city of Nicomedia. The flames had devastated a number of private residences, a public building, and the local temple of Isis. Pliny reports (*Ep.* 10.33) that one reason for the rapid spread of the fire had been the simple lack of buckets and fire engines, another the indolence of the locals. To prepare the city better for fires in the future he had therefore ordered the acquisition of suitable fire-fighting apparatus and, in the letter referenced above, requested the emperor's permission to set up a voluntary fire-fighting squad. Here, however, is Trajan's response,

> You are of opinion that it would be proper to establish a company (*collegium*) of firemen in Nicomedia on the model of what has been practised in several other cities. But it is to be remembered that societies of this sort have greatly disturbed the peace of the province in general, and of those cities in particular. Whatever name we give them, and for whatever purposes they may be founded, they will not fail to form themselves into factious assemblies, however short their meetings may be. It will therefore be safer to provide such machines as are of service in extinguishing fires, enjoining the owners of houses to assist in preventing the mischief from spreading, and, if it should be necessary, to call in the aid of the populace (*Ep.* 10.34; tr. Radice, LCL).

Trajan, of course, speaks specifically of the province under Pliny's government, but problems with riotous behaviour appear not to have

10 Cf. also C. R. Moss, *The Myth of Persecution: How Early Christians Invented a Story of Martyrdom* (New York, N.Y.: HarperOne, 2013), 163–87.

been limited to Pontus and Bithynia. In 59 CE, in Pompeii, due to rivalry between the locals and visitors from the neighbouring city of Nuceria, a massive riot broke out in connection with a gladiatorial show, organized by a local ex-senator. The unrest, according to Tacitus (*Ann.* 14.17), had been of such proportions that Pompeii had afterwards been barred from hosting similar shows for a full decade. And interestingly, Tacitus notes that the town's "*collegia*, which had been formed illegally" were simultaneously disbanded. This suggests that private *collegia* had played a pivotal role in the conflict, or at least were believed to have done so. No less tellingly, Tertullian claims, in *Apology* 38.2, that certain associations had been banned by the authorities "on a prudential regard to the public order, that the state may not be divided into parties, which would naturally lead to disturbance" (tr. Thelwall, ANF).[11]

Luke, however, was keen to demonstrate that Rome had nothing in that regard to fear from Christianity. Interestingly, he appears to have imagined that the world, including the Roman Empire, was in the hands of demonic forces,

> And he [the devil] led him up and showed him all the kingdoms of the world in a moment of time, and the devil said to him, "To you I will give all this authority and their glory, for it has been delivered to me (ὅτι ἐμοὶ παραδέδοται), and I give it to whom I please. If you, then, will worship me, it will all be yours." And Jesus answered him, "It is written, 'You shall worship the Lord your God, and him only shall you serve'" (4:5–8).

But he was careful to signal that the church's response to this (deplorable) state of affairs was neither open rebellion nor any other form of disturbance of the civic order. Luke indicates this in a number of ways throughout both of his writings. In the gospel, for instance, through his portrayal of Joseph's obedient response to Augustus' commandment

11 Cf. R. MacMullen, *Enemies of the Roman Order: Treason, Unrest, and Alienation in the Empire*, American Council of Learned Societies (Cambridge, MA: Harvard University Press, 1966), 167–78, and further W. Nippel, *Public Order in Ancient Rome*, Key Themes in Ancient History (Cambridge; New York, N.Y.: Cambridge University Press, 1995), 27–30.

ἀπογράφεσθαι πᾶσαν τὴν οἰκουμένην (2:1–4; contrast with Jos. *B.J.* 2.117–118; *AJ* 18.1–5), Jesus' explicit sanction of tax payment (20:20–26), and Pilate's threefold declaration of Jesus' innocence of among other things proclaiming himself king (23:4, 14, 22; cf. Mk 15:1–15; Mt. 27:11–26); in Acts through his descriptions of Paul's successful encounters with the Roman legal apparatus (e.g., 18:12–17; 26:32), his final demise in Rome notwithstanding (23:11; 25:11–12; 27:24), and of the consistently peaceful conduct of the missionaries, which sets them apart, for instance, from the inhabitants of Ephesus (19:23–40).

There is no need in this context to enter a detailed analysis of these various motifs. Luke's "apologetic" agenda has been adequately examined by other interpreters.[12] We may limit our comments to a brief discussion of why this agenda is there at all. We have seen that according to the classic understanding, the apologetic qualities of Luke's oeuvre reflect an ambition on his part to defend the church before the Roman authorities. This presumes a non-Christian readership for his work, a presumption that receives very little support from the work itself. The classic understanding is therefore almost certainly incorrect. Sterling has offered a modified version of this view. He proposes that Luke intended his work to serve as a sort of indirect apology in the sense that he wished for it to supply his readers with "examples and precedents" that testify to the church's political innocence on the basis of which they could then "make their own *apologia*" if they should one day find themselves in the dock.[13] This reading is possible, but presupposes that Luke had imagined a situation of violent conflict with the state to be on the horizon. This may seem unlikely, not least given his addition in 9:23 of the modifier καθ' ἡμέραν ("daily") to Mark's and Matthew's "If anyone would come after me, let him deny himself and *take up his cross* and follow me" (Mk 8:34; cf. Mt. 16:24). This addition reads most naturally as a "demartyrologization" of his sources, which could be seen to indicate that Luke had felt less of a need than Mark or Matthew to prepare his readers for a lethal confrontation with the authorities, and therefore chosen to reinterpret the act of "taking up one's cross" as signifying, rather than the acceptance of a vio-

12 See above all the superb exegesis in Rowe, *World Upside Down*, 53–89.

13 G. E. Sterling, *Historiography and Self-Definition: Josephos, Luke-Acts and Apologetic Historiography*, SNT 64 (New York, N.Y.: Brill, 1992), 380–86, esp. 386.

lent death (which can hardly be sustained καθ' ἡμέραν), something along the lines of a patient endurance of poverty, shame, and social isolation (see further chapter 3).

I have already hinted at my own solution to the problem, which is that Luke intended his "political apology" to render the Christian faith more appealing to Theophilus and thus to help cement his commitment to the congregation. If the social profile I have sketched of Theophilus as a prominent member of society and possibly even a holder of political office is correct, Luke could easily have expected him to respond approvingly to the message delivered in both Luke and Acts that Christianity did not imply disloyalty to the state and that the Christian movement was not a hotbed for rebels and disturbers of the peace. This was for two reasons: both because Theophilus himself would presumably have wished to continue regarding himself as a loyal citizen of Rome, and because rioters, political or not, were generally frowned upon by the members of the social grouping to which Theophilus belonged. As L. M. Wills has put it, "the Roman ruling classes stood in perpetual fear of rebellion," and those regarded as rebels were "viewed with hatred, fear, and loathing, evoking much the same reaction as do those today who are considered 'terrorists'" (cf., e.g., Polyb. 6.44; Sal. *Cat.* 38.1; Jos. *B.J.* 6.285–287; Tac. *Ann.* 1.16–32).[14] Theophilus could thus well be expected to appreciate learning that those were not the type of people that he would be associating with by committing himself fully to the church.

It is worth mentioning that the reading I am proposing here comes close to the one advanced by Ph. F. Esler about a quarter of a century ago. In his seminal monograph *Community and Gospel in Luke-Acts*, he wrote,

> There is only one answer which offers a satisfying explanation for the political theme in Luke-Acts, that among the members of Luke's community were a number of Romans serving the empire in a military or administrative capacity, and that part of Luke's task was to present Christian history in such a way as to demonstrate that faith in Jesus Christ and allegiance to Rome were not mutually inconsistent.[15]

14 Wills, "Depiction of the Jews," 635; cf. also MacMullen, *Enemies of the Roman Order*, 180–5.

15 Esler, *Community and Gospel*, 210.

Esler's proposal, however, differs from mine in two respects. First, of course, he speaks of "a number of Romans" and does not (unlike me) point specifically to Theophilus. Indeed, elsewhere in his book he explicitly discourages interpreters from focusing on this person: "Theophilus may or may not have been typical of the reading public for whom the work was intended; its readers may well have been different."[16] Second, he appears to presume that Luke had always been prepared to support those members of his community who were "serving the empire in a military or administrative capacity" in continuing to do so, whereas I suggest that when writing the first instalment of his oeuvre he was trying to induce Theophilus to adopt a lifestyle that would prevent this (see further chapters 3 and 4). However, in order to avoid causing unnecessary vexation on his part, and hence in order to avoid pushing him away, I propose he nevertheless tried to reassure Theophilus that this alternative lifestyle would not involve political infidelity to the empire and that—despite a widely held belief perhaps—the Christian church was not a breeding ground for insurrectionists.

We now turn to Luke's discourse on Christianity and novelty.

Christianity and novelty

In 1:21–28 Mark tells the story of how, at the beginning of his ministry, Jesus taught and healed in the synagogue at Capernaum. On the first Sabbath after his arrival in the town with his recently gathered group of disciples, he entered the local synagogue and started to preach. The audience was immediately struck with wonder, "For he taught them as one having authority, and not as the scribes" (1:22). When afterwards he performed an exorcism on one of the men present, the awe of the crowd intensified, "And they were all astounded, so that they discussed among themselves, saying, 'What is this? A new teaching with authority! He commands even the unclean spirits, and they obey him.' And straight away the news about him went out everywhere into all the surrounding region of Galilee" (1:27–28). In 4:31–37 in his gospel Luke gives us essentially the same story. Admittedly he places the episode at a different

16 Ibid., 24.

time, but apart from that the details of the narratives are nearly identical, except that, according to Luke, Jesus' audience did not describe his teaching as "new" (cf. Mk 1:27, διδαχὴ καινή). His version of the crowd's reaction to his instruction reads as follows, "They were all amazed and kept saying to one another, 'What kind of teaching is this (τίς ὁ λόγος οὗτος)? For he commands the unclean spirits with authority and power, and out they come!' And word about him began to reach every place in the region" (4:36–37).

Luke's redaction at this point is not accidental. It reveals a conscious effort on his part to eliminate the impression left behind by Mark, and to a lesser extent Matthew, of Christianity as "something new."[17] Luke admittedly twice allows the epithet of newness to stick to Christian teaching. In Luke 5:36–39 he retains Mark's (2:21–22) and Matthew's (9:16–17) parables of garments and wine and wineskins while even expanding slightly on the latter, both of which sayings associate Christianity with newness, even in their Lucan setting.[18] And in Luke 22:20, uniquely among the synoptics, he has Jesus identify the covenant he inaugurates through the giving of his blood as "the new covenant" (ἡ καινὴ διαθήκη) (cf. Mk 14:24; Mt. 26:28). Elsewhere, however, he proceeds by the logic of 4:36–37. In 22:7–23 he deletes Mark's (14:25) and Matthew's (26:29) mention of "new wine" (cf. αὐτό ... καινόν) to be imbibed in the realm of heaven. And in Acts 17:22–31, through the Areopagus sermon, he dismisses the classification of Christianity by certain Athenians as a καινή ... διδαχή (cf. 17:19), by suggesting through Paul that the Christian God had been worshipped in Athens prior to the missionary's arrival in the city—even if only "unknowingly" so (17:23)[19]—and that Christian doctrine intersects with various strands of pagan literature and philosophy (17:24–29).[20]

17 Ibid., 215–17.

18 Fitzmyer, *Luke I–IX*, 596–7; Johnson, *Luke*, 99–100; against Green, *Luke*, 249–50.

19 Cf. Rowe, *World Upside Down*, 27–41; C. K. Rowe, "The Grammar of Life: The Areopagus Speech and Pagan Tradition," *NTS* 57, no. 1 (2011): 31–50.

20 Cf. D. L. Balch, "The Areopagus Speech: An Appeal to the Stoic Historian Posidonius against Later Stoics and the Epicureans," in *Greeks, Romans, and Christians (FS Abraham Malherbe)*, ed. D. L. Balch et al. (Minneapolis, MN: Fortress Press, 1990), 52–79; J. H. Neyrey, "Acts 17, Epicureans, and Theodicy: A Study in Stereotypes,"

Later in this chapter we shall see that Luke's writings contain further manifestations of this determination to divorce Christianity from the notion of newness. At this point, however, we may appropriately ask ourselves whether this determination, like the one to portray Christianity as politically innocent, may be seen to reflect a wish on Luke's part to recast Christianity in a way that he thought might appeal to Theophilus. The answer can only be in the affirmative. In the fourth century BCE, Timaeus of Locri (94c) suggested that τὸ πρεσβύτερον κάρρον ἐστὶ τῶ νεωτέρω.[21] The sentiment expressed by these words—"the old is better than the new"—was nearly universally shared among Greeks and Romans of the privileged classes throughout antiquity (see, e.g., Plat. *Tim.* 22b; Cic. *Leg.* 2.10.27; *Nat. deo.* 3.1.5–4.10).[22]

Most elite Romans were suspicious of novelty and believed that virtue was to found only in the past, or in customs, practices, and institutions that were firmly rooted in the past; hence the profound yearning we find not least in the writings of the early empire for the *mos maiorum*, i.e., "the customs of the ancestors" (e.g., Liv. 1.*praef.11*; Val. Max. 2.1.1–7). Augustus' boast in the *Res gestae* of his achievements in the realm of family law clearly presumes this worldview, "Through the new laws passed on my proposal I have brought back many of the exemplary practices of our ancestors, which were falling into neglect" (*legibus novis me auctore latis multa exempla maiorum exolescentia iam ex nostro saeculo reduxi*)" (8.5).[23] The excerpt nicely illustrates that innovation was treasured by elite Romans (the emperor's intended audience) only to the extent that it was seen to constitute a revival of a glorious past.

Given their distrust of novelty, elite Romans would typically judge the worth of nations on the basis of their perceived age. Nations that were able to trace their origins back to a distant past would generally enjoy higher esteem than those with a short history. Roman writers

in *Greeks, Romans, and Christians (FS Abraham Malherbe)*, ed. D. L. Balch et al. (Minneapolis, MN: Fortress Press, 1990), 118–34.

21 Doric for τὸ πρεσβύτερον κρεῖττον ἐστὶ τοῦ νεωτέρου.

22 Cf. above all P. Pilhofer, *Presbyteron kreitton: Der Altersbeweis der jüdischen und christlichen Apologeten und seine Vorgeschichte*, WUNT 2.39 (Tübingen: Mohr Siebeck, 1990).

23 Tr. C. Edwards, *The Politics of Immorality in Ancient Rome* (Cambridge; New York, N.Y.: Cambridge University Press, 1993), 34.

were painfully aware of the relatively recent birth of their own nation, traditionally dated to 753 BCE, and would sometimes engage in attempts to push it further back. In the *Aeneid*, Vergil traced the origin of the Romans back to the time of the Trojan War. And Dionysius of Halicarnassus (*Ant. rom.* 1.4.1–11.4) tried to push it even further back into the past.[24] Similarly, Josephus' work reveals a sustained effort to establish the antiquity of the Jews. In *Histories* 5.2 Tacitus relates six theories about the origins of the Jews, many of which date them to a relatively recent period. The historian claims that the most commonly accepted view identifies the Jews as an offshoot of the Egyptian nation expelled from their country by the King Bocchoris (in the eighth century BCE) on account of their evident lack of divine favour. Josephus was familiar with some of these theories (e.g., *Apion* 1.2, 58, 2.15–21, 288) and attempted to systematically impugn them, clearly in order to establish the virtue of the Jews. In *Jewish Antiquities* he did this by tracing the origins of the Jews, through a translation of the Hebrew Bible, back to the time immediately after the world's creation; in *Against Apion* by citing what he perceived as "supporting evidence" of this view from the works of non-Jewish historians.[25]

If the profile I have drawn of Theophilus is correct, we may safely assume that he would have been mistrustful of things new and less inclined to commit himself to the church if he believed that its teaching was essentially καινή. It is therefore quite conceivable, if by no means certain, that Luke's attempt to dissociate Christianity from the notion of novelty betrays a resolution on his part to accommodate his portrayal of Jesus and the church to the "grammar" of his patron's thought, and thereby to convince him of the sagacity of his decision to join the Christian movement.

24 Mason, *Josephus and the New Testament*, 104.

25 The Graeco-Roman preference for antiquity was framed by a mythological conception of the history of the human species as a history of continual decay from the time of the Golden Age down to the present (Hes. *Op.* 105–99; Ov. *Met.* 1.89–150; Sen. *Ep.* 90); cf. ibid., 103. It is worth noting, with L. H. Feldman (*Jew and Gentile in the Ancient World: Attitudes and Interactions from Alexander to Justinian* [Princeton, N.J.: Princeton University Press, 1993], 178), that in his attack on Christianity the philosopher Celsus (ap. Or. *Cels.* 4.14) suggestively professed to have had "nothing new to say, only ancient doctrine."

Christianity and the Jews

In this final section of the chapter we shall turn our attention to Luke's discourse on the Jews. We shall discuss whether this, too, may be seen to reflect an attempt by Luke to adapt the image of Christianity to the preconceptions of his dedicatee. Luke's approach to the Jews and Judaism may seem slightly paradoxical. On the one hand, more than any of the other gospel writers, he posits continuity between Judaism and Christianity. On the other hand, however, he suggests that the Jews generally, though at first sympathetic to Christianity, eventually turned against it, and were therefore in the end excluded from the reach of God's salvation. I shall refer to these different aspects as "strand (a)" and "strand (b)," respectively. I realize that not everyone will agree entirely with my characterization of strand (b). That is, few would contest that Luke portrays the Jews as, in the end, generally hostile to Christianity, and even violently so. However, many have argued, despite the existence of certain indications to the contrary, that his text nevertheless communicates a vision of a future redemption of the Jews, or at least of some of them. I hope to be able to show in the course of the following analyses, however, that the description given here is accurate.

I shall open this section by summarizing the two strands outlined here. Then I will seek to explain why both of these strands "are there," despite the tension that one might perceive between them. Lastly I shall consider, on the basis of the explanation offered, whether Luke's treatment of Christianity and the Jews may in the end be seen as intended to reshape Christianity according to the presumptions of Theophilus.

Strand (a). If the characterization of strand (b) given above is somewhat controversial, that of strand (a) is not. Scholars universally agree that Luke was remarkably eager to emphasize the Jewish roots of Christianity. As a result, all that is needed here is a brief overview of some of the key passages to illustrate the point. In Luke 1:6, 8–25; 2:21–24, 41, for example, the author portrays the parents of both Jesus and John as pious law-abiding Jews, and the father of the latter as a priest of the Jerusalem temple. In 3:23–38 he traces the lineage of Jesus back to the patriarchs and beyond. In Acts 3:13 he speaks of the Christian God as the God of Abraham, Isaac, and Jacob. In 7:2–53 he allows Stephen to defend himself on charges of hostility to the law and the temple through a powerful retelling of Israel's past that effectively appropriates the history of the Jews for the Christian movement. Furthermore, at several moments he frames the ministry of Jesus as a realization of Jewish prophecy (e.g., Lk. 2:25–31, 38; 4:16–30). In Acts 2:16–21 he has Peter interpret the descent of the Spirit as a fulfilment of Joel 3:1–5 and in 15:15–18 James declare that the mission to the gentiles was initiated in accordance with God's will as expressed in Amos 9:11–12 (cf. Isa. 45:21). And in Acts 24:14 he portrays Paul as claiming to be serving the God of the ancestors and to believe in everything "laid down according to the law or written in the prophets." The list could easily be extended, but there is hardly any need.

Strand (b). Let us turn instead to the second strand. This develops the theme of what might be termed "the parting of the ways between Christianity and Judaism," to borrow a phrase from modern scholarship. We may summarize this strand by focusing first on Luke's portrayal of the Jews' response to Christianity and then on his description of the consequence of that response for their possibility of obtaining salvation.

I remarked above that, according to Luke, the Jews were originally sympathetic to the Christian movement. That is a slightly inaccurate statement because with few exceptions (Lk. 13:31; Acts 5:33–39; 6:7; 23:9; 50–56; 26:24–32) Luke portrays the Jewish leaders—i.e., the priests, the scribes, the kings, the members of the council, and the Pharisees—as hostile to Christianity from beginning to end. The comment does, however, fit his characterization of the people, i.e., of the "ordinary," "non-leading" Jews. In contrast to their leaders, these Jews initially respond favourably to Christianity, in Luke as well as in Acts. Thus, in Luke (except in 4:28–30) we find the people unanimously siding with Jesus up to the moment of the beginning of his passion, and several passages indicate that the Jewish leadership chose to have him killed—yet nevertheless also decided to postpone his actual arrest—precisely on account of the popularity he enjoyed among the general populace (19:47; 20:26; 22:1–6). Similarly, in Acts we learn that the people were initially sympathetic to the church. In the early days of the mission, during the so-called "Jerusalem springtime," conversions took place by the thousands (2:41; 4:4; 5:14), and even among non-converting Jews the disciples enjoyed considerable esteem (2:47; 4:21, 33).

In both Luke and Acts, however, most of the non-leading Jews eventually turn against the Christian movement. Thus, in Luke 22:47–53, in connection with the seizure of Jesus in Gethsemane, we suddenly find "the crowd" uniting with their leaders, and for the remainder of the gospel it remains on their side. In 23:1–5 and 18–25 it accuses Jesus before Pilate and demands his execution, and in 23:26–38, uniquely among the gospels, it even appears to physically perform his crucifixion.[26] Some Jews, in addition to his most immediate following, remain devoted to Jesus. In 23:27, just prior to his crucifixion, we learn that "a great number of the people (πολὺ πλῆθος τοῦ λαοῦ) followed him" among whom were certain "women who were beating their chest and wailing for him." And in 24:13–35, in the episode of the walk to Emmaus, we hear of two disciples who mourn and profess to have "hoped that he was the one to redeem Israel" (24:21). Yet these Jews appear to form a minority. In Acts, at least, we learn that it was *the* Jews, i.e., the Jews generally, one presumes, who were responsible for Jesus' death (2:14–39; 3:12–26; 7:52–53; 10:34–44; 13:16–41).

In Acts, the non-leading Jews are generally favourable to the church only up to the moment when the action taken against Stephen begins (6:8–8:1). Certainly, scattered conversions of Jews continue to take place throughout the remainder of the narrative (9:35, 42; 14:1; 17:4, 11; 18:8; cf. 13:43; 18:20; 19:17), but from this moment on Jewish rejection appears to be the norm, and the members of the people frequently emerge as enemies of the church on a par with their leaders. In 6:12 and 7:57–59, "ordinary" Jews throw themselves on Stephen, drag him before the council, and stone him to death. In 8:1 they persecute the church. On several occasions they oppose Paul during his mission in the diaspora (13:6–11, 45, 50; 14:1–4; 17:5–9, 13; 18:6, 12; 19:9; 20:3; 28:24), often resorting to

26 Cf. L. Gaston, "Anti-Judaism and the Passion Narrative in Luke and Acts," in *Anti-Judaism in Early Christianity. Vol. 1: Paul and the Gospels*, ed. P. Richardson and D. Granskou, Studies in Christianity and Judaism 2 (Waterloo, ON: Wilfrid Laurier University Press, 1986), 149–50; J. T. Sanders, *The Jews in Luke-Acts* (London: SCM Press, 1987), 9–13; Mason, *Josephus and the New Testament*, 270.

rioting and violent conduct. Once they nearly even murder him (14:19; cf. also 9:23). And in 21:27, after his return to Jerusalem, Jews from Asia arouse the crowds, which then seek to kill him (21:31; 23:12). General Jewish hostility to the church is furthermore evident in such passages as 12:11; 18:28; 21:11, 36; 22:30; 23:27; 24:9; 25:2, 7; 26:17, 21; 28:19; and in 12:3; 24:27; 25:9, where political or military power holders detain or mistreat members of the church in order to curry favour with "the Jews." In 21:20 we admittedly hear that the Christian community in Jerusalem had increased during Paul's absence and thus come to comprise "thousands of Jews." But even these Jews are sceptical of Paul (21:21) and do nothing to protect him once he is attacked by "the Jews" on the temple square (21:27–32), or to defend him after he is arrested by the commander Claudius Lysias (21:33).

In sum we may say that whereas Luke hardly paints a uniform picture of the Jews, he does suggest that the Jewish leaders were generally opposed to the Christian movement from start to finish and that, both in the course of Jesus' own ministry and that of his followers, most of the Jewish people eventually followed suit, after initially having been favourable to it.

In the early chapters of Luke we learn that the birth of Jesus was intended to bring salvation to both Jews and gentiles. Most notably, perhaps, in 2:29–32 the pious Simeon gives thanks to God on seeing the infant Jesus along the following lines,

> Master, now you are dismissing your servant in peace,
> According to your word;
> For my eyes have seen your salvation,
> Which you have prepared in the presence of all peoples,
> A light for revelation to the gentiles (φῶς εἰς ἀποκάλυψιν ἐθνων)
> And for glory to your people Israel (καὶ δόξαν λαοῦ σου Ἰσραήλ).
> (Cf. also 1:67–79; 2:36–38; 3:6)

As we have seen, however, most of the Jews eventually rejected Jesus. In consequence, at the end of his work (in Acts 28:25–28), Luke declares, through Paul in Rome, that the Jews have therefore now disqualified themselves from God's salvation and that in future the offer of redemption will be extended only to people of gentile origin. After a couple of largely unsuccessful meetings with the Jews in Rome, Paul hurls the following condemnation at them,

> The Holy Spirit spoke rightly (καλῶς) to your ancestors through the prophet Isaiah [6:9–10],
> "Go to this people and say,
> You will indeed listen, but never understand,
> And you will indeed look, but never perceive.
> For this people's heart has grown dull,
> And their ears are hard of hearing,
> And they have closed their eyes;
> So that they may never look with their eyes,
> And listen with their ears, and understand with their heart
> And turn—and I would heal them."
> Let it be known to you therefore that this salvation of God (τοῦτο τὸ σωτήριον τοῦ θεοῦ) has been sent to the gentiles; they will listen (αὐτοὶ καὶ ἀκούσονται).

Although the salvation of God was initially intended for "all flesh" (3:6), it will now be available only for gentiles; and unlike the (vast majority of the) Jews, "they will listen."[27] Prior to the moment of Paul's arrival in Rome, of course, numerous Jews had embraced Christianity and enrolled in the community of faith. These Jews, Paul implies, will remain within the reach of God's σωτήριον. But for everyone else, the window of opportunity has closed. In Luke's narrative world, from this moment on, the parting of the ways between Christianity and Judaism, and indeed between the Christians and the Jews, was thus an irreversible reality. And the way of the Jews would lead to perdition.

A certain tension undeniably exists between Luke 1:67–79; 2:29–32, 36–38; 3:6, on the one hand, and Acts 28:25–28, on the other. This tension could be taken to suggest that in the latter passage Paul expresses himself in a way that disagrees with God's plan. Two factors, however, need to

27 L. T. Johnson (*The Acts of the Apostles*, SP 5 [Collegeville, MI: Liturgical Press, 1992], 472) rightly notes that "[t]he use of the intensive pronoun *autoi* marks a sharp contrast to the disbelieving Jews: *they* will believe."

be taken into account. First, Luke clearly suggests that when Paul finally denounced the Jews he did so only after the Jews had been offered multiple chances for redemption. In Acts 2:22–41 and 3:12–26, for instance, Peter reminds the Jews in Jerusalem of their shared guilt in Jesus' death, but nevertheless offers them an opportunity for reconciliation. Similarly, in the diaspora, Paul twice resumes his mission to the Jews after having announced his resolve to leave them and "go to the gentiles" instead (13:46, in Pisidian Antioch; 18:6, in Corinth)—in both cases, admittedly, only in new cities. Luke thus leaves his readers with the impression that when he eventually dismissed the Jews, he and the other missionaries had done everything in their power to show compassion and bring them around. Thus, although initially they had been promised otherwise, Luke clarifies that the Jews only had themselves to blame for their final demise. Certainly, the missionaries were free of guilt.

Second, several utterances by Jesus suggest that the Jews' eventual rejection of the gospel and their subsequent downfall were always anticipated in heaven and part of a divine plan. In Luke 4:24–27, before having encountered any form of Jewish opposition, Jesus thus predicts that he will be rejected by his own and that his ministry will benefit only people of a gentile origin. Likewise, in 10:13–16 he condemns the towns of Galilee on account of disbelief, before any general opposition to his work has actually materialized. Similar predictions figure in 13:25–30; 19:41–44; 21:20–28 and possibly in 13:34–35, most of which passages I shall return to and comment on later. Accordingly, despite the tension that clearly exists between the opening chapters of Luke's gospel and the closing verses of Acts, Luke's narrative leaves the reader assured that Paul's condemnation of the Jews in Rome was both fully justified, given the Jews' continual acts of obstinacy, and in accordance with God's foreknowledge and design.

Around half a century ago, E. Haenchen suggested that in Acts 28:25–28 Luke should be taken to have "written the Jews off."[28] It will be clear from what I have said that I agree with this position, as do,

28 Haenchen, "Book of Acts as Source Material," 278; cf. E. Haenchen, "Judentum und Christentum in der Apostelgeschichte," *ZNW* 54 (1963): 183–7.

incidentally, several other interpreters.[29] As noted, however, despite the apparent harshness of Paul's words in these verses, numerous scholars believe that Luke's text heralds a future restoration either of the people as a whole or of certain individual Jews. I shall take some time here to review the most important arguments that have been advanced in favour of this position. I shall conclude, however, that none of them are convincing.

(i) As recently mentioned, twice prior to Acts 28:25–28 Paul declares his intention to abandon the Jews and go to the gentiles (13:46; 18:6). In both cases, he nevertheless quickly resumes the Jewish mission, albeit in both cases only in new cities. Some scholars detect a pattern here and propose that Luke intended us to imagine that Paul would likewise resume his work among the Jews at some point after Acts 28:25–28, if not in Rome then elsewhere.[30] If that is true, then certainly it would seem that Luke had imagined the salvation of God to have remained available to the Jews after Acts 28:28, at least to some of them.

Theoretically, this reading is possible. As J. B. Tyson has pointed out, however, it seems considerably more likely that 13:46 and 18:6 should be read in the light of 28:25–28 than the other way around:

> [D]ue to its location at the end of Luke-Acts, the third announcement carries special weight. It functions as the culminating announcement, justification for which draws not only on Paul's immediate experience in Rome, but also on those previous occasions of Jewish

29 Gaston, "Anti-Judaism and the Passion Narrative"; Sanders, *Jews in Luke-Acts*, 298–9; J. T. Sanders, "The Jewish People in Luke-Acts," in *Luke-Acts and the Jewish People: Eight Perspectives*, ed. J. B. Tyson (Minneapolis, MN: Augsburg, 1988), 51–75; H. Räisänen, "The Redemption of Israel: A Salvation-Historical Problem in Luke-Acts," in *Luke-Acts: Scandinavian Perspectives*, ed. P. Luomanen, Publications of the Finnish Exegetical Society 54 (Göttingen: Vandenhoeck & Ruprecht, 1991), 94–114; Wills, "Depiction of the Jews"; M. P. Bonz, "Luke's Revision of Paul's Reflection in Romans 9–11," in *Early Christian Voices: In Texts, Traditions, and Symbols (FS François Bovon)*, ed. D. H. Warren, A. G. Brock, and D. W. Pao, Biblical Interpretation Series 66 (Boston, MS: Brill, 2003), 143–51; Pervo, *Dating Acts*, 345–6.

30 R. L. Brawley, *Luke-Acts and the Jews: Conflict, Apology, and Conciliation*, SBLMS 33 (Atlanta, GA: Scholars Press, 1987), 68–78; Tannehill, *Narrative Unity: Acts*, 350–1; J. D. G. Dunn, *The Acts of the Apostles*, Epworth Commentaries (Valley Forge, PN: Trinity Press International, 1996), 353.

> rejection. The announcements at Pisidian Antioch and Corinth now turn out to be anticipations of this final proclamation of the termination of the Pauline mission to the Jews.[31]

Tyson's analysis is convincing by itself (except that I would add that 13:46 and 18:6 not only anticipate, but also justify 28:25–28; cf. above), but may receive further support from the following two observations. First, in 13:46 and 18:6, unlike in 28:25–28, Paul does not dismiss the Jews generally, but only the particular Jews he is addressing. Second, in Pisidian Antioch and Corinth Paul speaks only of taking his own mission away from the Jews; in Rome, by contrast, he speaks rather more radically of a transfer, or a sending, of God's σωτήριον.

(ii) I noted above that in 28:25–28 Luke should hardly be seen to deprive those Jews who had committed themselves to Christianity prior to Paul's arrival in Rome of access to God's salvation. These Jews, apparently, had somehow been able to "resist" the prophecy of Isaiah 6:9–10. Some scholars propose that Luke should therefore also be seen to have been open to the possibility that certain Jews of the future would do the same, and hence in similar fashion be able to render themselves worthy of salvation. According to this view, Luke intended Paul's denouncement of the Jews in 28:25–28 to apply only to those particular Jews who had either rejected Christ in the past or would do so in the future.[32]

One could certainly argue that Luke ought to have held such a view. Anything else might seem unfair. Yet nothing suggests that he did. The force of his rhetoric is clear. Those whom Paul condemns are *the* people, not any particular *part* of the people. And surely Paul's concluding remark in 28:28 that the salvation of God had been "sent to the gentiles" would appear meaningless, if what he meant to communicate was that this salvation had in fact remained available to the Jews exactly in the manner it had always been.

31 J. B. Tyson, *Images of Judaism in Luke-Acts* (Columbia, S.C.: University of South Carolina Press, 1992), 177–8; cf. Sanders, *Jews in Luke-Acts*, 298–9; Marguerat, *First Christian Historian*, 224–5; Pervo, *Acts*, 681.

32 E.g., Tannehill, *Narrative Unity: Acts*, 351; Tyson, *Images of Judaism*, 174–8.

An objection, however, presents itself. If we hold that in 28:25–28 Paul condemns the people as a whole, does it not follow that he condemns also those Jews who had accepted the faith prior to the moment of this announcement of his? Interestingly, Luke seems to have been aware of this problem and tried to avoid it. Thus, in 28:25 he remarkably allows Paul to speak to the Roman Jews of "your ancestors" (τοὺς πατέρας ὑμῶν) instead of "our ancestors," as certainly one could have expected given his own ethnic origin. Through this rather peculiar use of pronouns, Luke, I suspect, was trying to suggest that those Jews who had joined the Christian movement prior to 28:25–28 (cf. also 7:51–52) had in some manner ceased to be members of the Jewish people. In that way he could ensure that Paul's condemnation in these verses could be taken to apply to all members of the Jewish people without backfiring on those who were already enrolled in the community of the church.

(iii) Immediately after Paul's denunciation of the Jews in 28:25–28, in 28:30, we learn that Paul remained in Rome "for two whole years in his own rented home (ἐν ἰδίῳ μισθώματι) and welcomed everyone who came to him (καὶ ἀπεδέχετο πάντας τοὺς εἰσπορευομένους πρὸς αὐτόν)." To the word πάντας the Western manuscript tradition (614, 2147 [gig p] vg^{mss} sy^{h**}) adds "Jew and Greek" (Ἰουδαίους τε καὶ Ἕλληνας). No one takes this form to be original, but several scholars believe that it accurately reflects the intended import of 28:30. Barrett, for instance, writes, "πάντας τοὺς εἰσπορευομένους ... would certainly not exclude either Jews or Gentiles. πάντας is important to Luke, and his meaning (though not his text) is rightly given by the Western insertion."[33] The presence of the term πάντας, according to this view, should thus be taken to signal that Paul had left the door open for the Jews and that salvation had remained attainable to them.

This reading requires that 28:25–28 should be read in the light of 13:46 and 18:6 and even that after 28:25–28 Paul should have been

33 C. K. Barrett, *A Critical and Exegetical Commentary on the Acts of the Apostles. Vol. 2: Introduction and Commentary on Acts XV–XXVIII*, ICC 34 (Edinburgh: T. & T. Clark, 1998), 1252; cf. also Cassidy, *Society and Politics*, 129–30; Tyson, *Images of Judaism*, 174–8; Tannehill, *Narrative Unity: Acts*, 351; Dunn, *Acts*, 353; Marguerat, *First Christian Historian*, 150–1; J. A. Fitzmyer, *The Acts of the Apostles: A New Translation with Introduction and Commentary*, AB 31 (New Haven, CN; London: Yale University Press, 1998), 797.

more lenient to the Jews than he had been after 13:46 and 18:6; for as we have seen, in the latter two cases he resumes his mission to the Jews only in new cities,[34] whereas in the former he would then be resuming it in the very same city in which he had denounced them. Since we have already seen that 13:46 and 18:6 should presumably be assessed in the light of 28:25–28 rather than the other way around, and since nothing in 28:25–28, or elsewhere in the immediate context, signals leniency, the reading appears improbable. Luke most likely understood πάντας to include only gentiles.

(iv). In its original setting, the prophecy of Isaiah 6:9–10 cited by Paul in 28:26–27 had served as a call for repentance, not as a message of denunciation. According to some interpreters,[35] we may therefore assume that Luke had intended to use the prophecy to a similar end and attempted, through Acts 28:25–28, to reach out to the Jews of his own time and move them to contrition. If that is true, of course, Luke could hardly be seen to have given up on the Jews.

This reading would have been persuasive had it not been for the fact that Luke's particular handling of the text suggests that he did not wish to use it according to its original purpose. On the contrary, the "Let it be known to you *therefore* (οὖν), etc." of Acts 28:28 suggests that he wished to use it instead as a scriptural justification for "writing the Jews off."

(v) In Luke 13:34–35 Jesus laments over Jerusalem,

34 Rowe (*World Upside Down*, 57) denies this. In his analysis of Acts 18:6 he argues that "Paul's response to the his Jewish opposition—'from now on I will go to the Gentiles' (v. 6)—is intentionally more provocative than programmatic, as his first move is in fact to take up residence next door to the synagogue and convert the ἀρχισυνάγωγος (with his household)." Rowe's reading, though, slightly distorts the text. The fact that Luke speaks of Crispus as having "come to believe" (ἐπίστευσεν) in Christ before noting, in the very same verse (18:8), that "many of the Corinthians who heard (ἀκούοντες) Paul became believers (ἐπίστευον) and were baptized" suggests that Crispus had not been among those who "heard" Paul after he had turned his back on the Jews, but had rather come to believe on the basis of what he had heard from Paul's mouth prior to that moment. Luke does not portray Paul as having actually preached to and thus actively converted Crispus after having dismissed the Jews.

35 D. P. Moessner, "Paul in Acts: Preacher of Eschatological Repentance to Israel," *NTS* 34, no. 1 (1988): 101–3; Dunn, *Acts*, 353.

> Jerusalem, Jerusalem, [the city] that kills the prophets and stones those who are sent to it! How often have I desired to gather your children together as a hen gathers her brood under her wings, and you were not willing! See, your house is left to you. And I tell you, you will not see me until the time comes when you say (οὐ μὴ ἴδητέ με ἕως εἴπητε),[36] "Blessed is the one who comes in the name of the Lord."

According to some interpreters, Jesus' prediction at the end of this section ("And I tell you, you will not, etc.") offers "a glimmer of hope" for the Jewish people.[37] Superficially, the prediction seems to be fulfilled in Luke 19:38, when Jesus is hailed at his entrance into Jerusalem precisely with the words, "Blessed is the king who comes in the name of the Lord," a near-quotation of the Septuagint Psalm 117:26. However, those who greet Jesus with these words on that occasion are his disciples, not the Jerusalemites, as Jesus' prediction would lead us to expect. Thus, technically speaking, Jesus' prophecy in 13:35 is not fulfilled at this point; and neither is it fulfilled anywhere else in the course of Luke's narrative.

Some commentators hold that Jesus' prophecy must therefore be taken to apply to an event after the end of Luke's narrative—the Parousia. What Jesus predicts in 13:35, then, is that the residents of Jerusalem will not come to see him until at the end of days, when he will return from heaven "in a cloud with power and great glory" (Lk. 21:27; cf. Dan 7:13). At that moment, it is argued, they will greet him with the words of Septuagint Psalm 117:26. And since that greeting implies faith (cf. 19:38), the prophecy implies that at this point the Jerusalemites—who operate here as a synecdoche for the Jewish people as a whole—will have turned and hence become worthy of salvation.[38]

36 Following 𝔓[75] I leave out ἥξει ὅτε, attested in 𝔓[45], ℵ, D, and numerous other witnesses. Exegetically the choice makes little difference.

37 V. Fusco, "Luke-Acts and the Future of Israel," *NovT* 38, no. 1 (1996): 11.

38 Marshall, *Luke*, 577; D. L. Bock, *Proclamation from Prophecy and Pattern: Lucan Old Testament Christology*, JSOTsup 12 (Sheffield: JSOT Press, 1987), 121; C. A. Evans, "Prophecy and Polemic: Jews in Luke's Scriptural Polemic," in *Luke and Scripture: The Function of Sacred Tradition in Luke-Acts*, ed. C. A. Evans and J. A. Sanders (Minneapolis, MN: Fortress Press, 1993), 178–9; M. L. Strauss, *The Davidic Messiah*

Two questions, however, need to be raised in response to this reading. (a) Did Luke intend for the prediction of 13:35 to apply to the Parousia? And (b) if he did, did he mean for it to communicate a message of hope? With respect to (a), one may certainly object that although in connection with his entrance into the city the Jerusalemites do not greet him according to the prophecy of 13:35, they do nevertheless see him (cf. οὐ μὴ ἴδητε). Thus, in a sense the most natural solution to the problem of the link between 13:35 and 19:38 is to infer either that the latter text proved Jesus' prophecy wrong, or that εἴπητε ("you say") in the former verse should be seen as a misprint for, e.g., εἴπωσι ("they say" or "some say"). One could, however, perceive 13:35 as an oracle about the eschaton (and thereby avoid the contradiction between 13:35 and 19:38) by construing the verb "see" in 13:35 metaphorically as "comprehend" or "recognize" (cf. LSJ, "ὁράω," III). On such a reading, Luke would be suggesting that although the Jerusalemites had certainly seen Jesus *visually* during the period of his earthly ministry after 13:35, they had not seen him *mentally*, i.e., had not actually fathomed his true identity. At the moment of the Parousia, however, they would, and at that point accordingly salute him the way his disciples had done at his entrance into the city.

This leads us to the answer to question (b). As noted, the greeting of Septuagint Psalm 117:26 implies faith. Thus, on the assumption that 13:35 does refer to the eschaton, there can be no doubt that the prophecy foretells that when Jesus returns in power and glory the Jerusalemites will salute him in a way that betrays acknowledgement of his true nature. The question, however, is: will this acknowledgement, or faith, according to Luke, be sufficient for them to attain redemption? Probably not. Let us recall that in order to read 13:35 as an oracle about the Parousia we must interpret ἴδητε metaphorically as a reference to mental sight, i.e., understanding and belief. Thus, on an eschatological reading, what Jesus predicts in 13:35 is that the Jerusalemites will not comprehend Jesus and believe in him until—ἕως—he returns "in a cloud" to pass judgment on the world. It is important to notice that syntactically his

in Luke-Acts: Promise and Its Fulfillment in Lukan Christology, JSNTsup 110 (Sheffield: JSOT Press, 1995), 315–7; Fusco, "Future of Israel," 10–13.

prediction cannot be taken to designate a future conversion by the Jerusalemites (and the Jews generally) prior to the event of the second coming.

In that light it is worth noting that according to at least some trends in Luke's cultural milieu this type of eleventh-hour conversion was not sufficient to save the penitent from eschatological doom.[39] *1 Enoch* points in this direction. In chapter 48 we learn that at the eschaton, when the Son of Man—intriguingly described there as "the light of the gentiles" (48.4)[40]—will arrive, "all who dwell on earth shall fall down and worship before him, and will glorify and bless and celebrate with song the Name of the Lord of spirits" (48.5). All the same, "he will preserve" only "the portion of the righteous" (48.7). The "kings of the earth" and "the strong who occupy the land" will be led off to destruction, "for they have denied the Lord of spirits and the Anointed One" (48.8–10). So 48.5 implies that although the members of this group will in fact be condemned, they will nevertheless take part in the glorification of the Messiah when he arrives (cf. the "all"). Chapters 62–63 confirm this. In chapter 62 we hear that the kings of the earth "shall stand up" and see the Son of Man "and recognize him, because he sits on the throne of his glory" (62.3).

> And all the mighty kings and the exalted and those who rule the earth
> Shall fall down before him on their faces,
> And worship and set their hope on that Son of Man
> And petition him and supplicate for mercy from him
> It will all be to no avail, however. For
> The Lord of spirits shall then so affright them
> That they shall hastily go forth from his presence,
> And their faces shall be filled with shame,
> And the darkness shall grow deeper on their faces.
> And he will deliver them to the angels of punishment
> (62.9–11)

39 Wolter, *Lukasevangelium*, 499.

40 Tr. M. Black, *The Book of Enoch, Or, I Enoch: A New English Edition. With Commentary and Textual Notes*, SVTP 7 (Leiden: Brill, 1985), 49–61, also of the following excerpts.

In chapter 63 the author recounts an interlude in the punishment of the mighty during which they collectively "confess their sins" (63.2) and "bless and glorify the Lord of spirits":

> Blessed is the Lord of spirits and the Lord of kings,
> And the Lord of the mighty and the Lord of the exalted,
> And the Lord of glory and the Lord of wisdom, etc.
> (63.2)

They then implore the Messiah for a moment's respite to glorify him further, but are rejected and once again dragged down into the flames of Sheol (63.5–12).

No one would doubt that the greetings offered to the Son of Man in these chapters betray an acknowledgement on the part of the mighty of his true identity—a belief in him, one might say. Yet this belief has no salutary effect, presumably because it arose only in connection with his final glorious manifestation. *1 Enoch* 48 and 62–63 therefore clarify that even if Luke 13:35 does operate as an oracle about the eschaton, we have no a priori reason to interpret it as portending a message of hope for the Jerusalemites. On the contrary, given the conspicuous similarities between Luke 13:35 and, e.g., *1 Enoch* 62.2 it seems rather more natural to read the prediction as a subtle prophetic announcement of their eschatological doom.[41] At the end of time, when Jesus returns from heaven, the Jerusalemites (and the Jews generally, if indeed they do work as a synecdoche) will greet him with words signifying faith and submission; "but then," as T. W. Manson notes, "it will be too late."[42] This understanding gains credence from the fact that only a few verses earlier in Luke's narrative Jesus predicts that "once the owner of the

41 The contention of Fusco ("Future of Israel," 13) that 13:35 cannot be read as a prophecy of the future condemnation of the Jerusalemites/Jews, since "the acclamation 'Blessed is the one who comes in the name of the Lord!' does not only proclaim Jesus' Messiahship; it also welcomes him with joy and thanksgiving" overlooks the similarly welcoming and joyful tone of 1 En 63.2–3.

42 T. W. Manson, *The Sayings of Jesus, as Recorded in the Gospels According to St. Matthew and St. Luke* (London: SCM Press, 1949), 128; cf. also J. A. Fitzmyer, *The Gospel According to Luke (X–XXIV): Introduction, Translation, and Notes*, AB 28A (Garden City, N.Y.: Doubleday, 1983), 1035–6.

house has got up and shut the door," i.e., once at the end of time God has barred the entrance into the kingdom of heaven, the Jews (who alone can claim that "we ate and drank in your presence, and you taught in our streets") will be left outside the edifice begging to gain entrance—but be rejected (13:25–27).

In sum, one is hard pressed to find in 13:35 an expression of hope for a future restoration of the Jews. Either the prediction in that verse does not relate to the Parousia at all (in which case it is either fulfilled or proved wrong in 19:38), or it does, but should then most likely be seen as an allusion to the Jews' final condemnation.

(vi). In Luke 21:20–24 Jesus predicts the destruction and further suffering of Jerusalem:

> When you see Jerusalem surrounded by armies, then know that its desolation has come near. Then those in Judea must flee to the mountains, and those inside the city must leave it, and those out in the country must not enter it; for these are days of vengeance, as a fulfillment of all that is written. Woe to those who are pregnant and to those who are nursing infants in those days! For there will be great distress on the earth and anger against this people; they will fall by the edge of the sword and be taken away as captives among all nations; and Jerusalem will be trampled on by the gentiles, until the times of the gentiles are fulfilled (ἄχρι οὗ πληρωθῶσιν καιροὶ ἐθνῶν).

According to some interpreters, the temporal limit that Luke assigns in 21:24c to the trampling of Jerusalem by gentiles communicates a vision of a future restoration of the city, and hence, perhaps, of the Jewish people. In Jewish prophetic literature the destruction of Jerusalem is often visualized as a just punishment for Jewish disbelief. This literature, however, generally perceives this destruction (which is typically performed by gentile military powers) as a temporary measure that will eventually yield to a glorious restitution (Zech. 12:1–14:21; Tob. 14:3–7; 2 *Bar.* 68:1–5). Scholars such as A. W. Wainwright, D. L. Tiede, Tannehill, Fusco, and Wolter propose that Luke's addendum in 21:24c indicates that he conceptualized the destruction and trampling of

Jerusalem in 70 CE onwards in much the same manner. Jerusalem had to suffer for its rejection of Jesus, and would have to do so for a certain while longer.[43] But at some moment either before or at Jesus' return (vividly portrayed in the following verses) the city will be liberated from its gentile oppressors. And this will signify that the Jews will then have been reconciled with heaven. God's punishment, the prediction implies, "will not last forever."[44]

This construction of 21:24c, however, collides with its immediate context. In 21:28 Jesus informs his disciples that once the signs of the end of the world begin to appear, *they* specifically may raise their heads in confidence that *their* redemption will then be drawing near (cf. ἐγγίζει ἡ ἀπολύτρωσις ὑμῶν). Interestingly, Jesus offers his disciples this word of reassurance after in 21:20–27 having carefully contrasted them with Jerusalem. This hardly invites us to imagine that Jerusalem will then in fact come to share in their redemption. I suggest that Luke added 21:24c, not because he wished to herald a future restoration of Jerusalem, but because doing so enabled him to visualize a period of absolute chaos prior to the return of Jesus. The scenario he develops may be summarized as follows. From the destruction of the temple until the end of the "times of the gentiles," Jerusalem will suffer at the hands of the gentiles (21:20–24). During this period the gentiles (i.e., the Romans) will serve as God's punitive instruments. This era, however, will come to an end and be replaced by a phase during which a cluster of cosmic disasters will unfold and "distress among nations on the earth" (ἐπὶ τῆς γῆς συνοχὴ ἐθνῶν) emerges, and "people faint from fear and foreboding of what is coming on the world" (ἀποψυχόντων ἀνθρώπων ἀπὸ φόβου καὶ προσδοκίας τῶν ἐπερχομένων τῇ οἰκουμένῃ) (21:25–26).[45] Naturally, during this period, Jerusalem will not be oppressed by the gentiles since they

43 A. W. Wainwright, "Luke and the Restoration of the Kingdom to Israel," *ExpTim* 89 (78 1977): 76–79; D. L. Tiede, *Prophecy and History in Luke-Acts* (Philadelphia, PA: Fortress Press, 1980), 93; R. C. Tannehill, "Israel in Luke-Acts: A Tragic Story," *JBL* 104, no. 1 (1985): 84–85; Fusco, "Future of Israel," 14; Wolter, *Lukasevangelium*, 678–9.

44 Fusco, "Future of Israel," 14.

45 Like Green (*Luke*, 740), I take these verses to refer to events that are sequentially posterior to those described in vv. 20–24.

themselves will be paralyzed with fear and hence incapable of dominating anyone. This hardly means, however, that Jerusalem will escape calamity, for the passage seems to imply that once the καιροὶ ἐθνῶν have come to an end, the Jerusalemites, too, will be seized by anguish and perplexity. Ἀνθρώπων in 21:26 should presumably be taken as an ethnically inclusive designation that disregards only those few individuals who "have embraced the project of God unveiled in Jesus' ministry and oriented themselves around the divine purpose," as Green puts it, and whose redemption is accordingly mentioned in 21:28.[46] Like Luke 13:35, 21:24c thus hardly extends a hope for Jerusalem or for the Jews generally. Insofar as they are concerned, the verse suggests only that at some point in the future their sufferings at the hands of the Romans will yield to another kind of suffering, which incidentally they will be sharing with everyone else doomed for perdition.

(vii) Throughout Luke's narrative both Jesus and his followers exhibit a remarkable degree of loyalty to the Jewish law (see, e.g., Lk. 16:17; Acts 10: 9–16, 34–35; 16:1–3; 21:26; 23:5; 24:14, 17–18; 25:8; 28:17).[47] Some commentators hold that Luke's decision to portray them in this manner can only be explained if we assume that he was addressing an ethnically mixed congregation and was anxious to describe the history of the church in a way that would bolster the confidence of its Jewish members, "whose grip on the gospel was under threat on account of criticism from Jews, or from conservative Jewish Christians, that they were endanger-

46 Ibid., 741.

47 Esler (*Community and Gospel*, 129) correctly dismisses Wilson's assessment (*Luke and the Law*, SNTSMS 50 [Cambridge: Cambridge University Press, 1983], 54–58) that Luke's outlook on the law should be "ambiguous" or "ambivalent." It has been suggested that at the Jerusalem council (Acts 15:7–29) the apostles are portrayed as abolishing or at least softening the law (Conzelmann, *Theology of St. Luke*, 147; C. Blomberg, "The Law in Luke-Acts," *JSNT* 22 [1984]: 53–80; J. H. Neyrey, "The Symbolic Universe of Luke-Acts," in *The Social World of Luke-Acts: Models for Interpretation*, ed. J. H. Neyrey [Peabody, MS: Hendrickson Publishers, 1991], 294). Nothing could be further from the truth. No one at that meeting even raises the possibility that Jewish Christians should cease to be subject to the law, or even parts of it; cf. M. Thiessen, *Contesting Conversion: Genealogy, Circumcision, and Identity in Ancient Judaism and Christianity* (Oxford: Oxford University Press, 2011), 111, 140–1.

ing the Jewish *ethnos* and the Mosaic law."[48] If that is true, it hardly makes sense to imagine that Luke should in fact have "written the Jews off."

But is the assumption of a mixed community the only viable explanation for Luke's discourse on the law? Given the deprecatory portrayal of the Jews in the latter parts of his works, the scenario of a mixed audience is hard to take in. Certainly, Luke does little to capture the goodwill of any Jewish readers. Fortunately, another explanation is available. We noted above that through his portrayal of the missionary activity of Peter and Paul, Luke leaves his readers with the impression that the Jews had received several chances for repentance when they were finally denounced. By so doing he clarifies that the Jews were themselves responsible for their exclusion from God's σωτήριον and the fateful parting of the ways. I believe that this was an important point for Luke to make, and shall explain why in due course. At the present moment I shall mention only that Luke's emphasis on Jesus' and the missionaries' loyalty to the law may well be seen to play into this motif. Had Jesus and the missionaries abandoned the law, and even encouraged other Jews to follow suit (cf. Acts 21:21), the Jews' opposition to the gospel could have seemed justified, even to a gentile audience, since in the Roman world neglect of one's inherited customs was generally regarded as impiety (Sen. ap. Aug. *Civ.* 6.10; Tac. *Hist* 5.4–5; Cels. ap. Or. *Cels.* 5.25–26). In that case, Jesus and his followers could have been viewed as at least indirectly accountable for the Jews' eventual rejection of the message and hostility to the church. As it is, however, they did not. Quite the opposite, besides remaining themselves loyal to the law, the disciples exerted themselves to ensure that even non-Jewish Christians would not cause Jews any offence through contraventions of the law (cf. Acts 15:21; 16:3).[49] So, just as the Jews were given numerous chances for redemption throughout the early days of Christianity, they were given no pretext for rejection of the message. Luke's discourse on the law need not therefore imply the existence of a mixed congregation, let alone any ambition on his part to reshape Christianity according to the needs of any Jewish

48 Esler, *Community and Gospel*, 129.

49 For the non-Jewish identity of Timothy see S. J. D. Cohen, *The Beginnings of Jewishness: Boundaries, Varieties, Uncertainties*, Hellenistic Culture and Society 31 (Berkeley, CA: University of California Press, 1999), 263–307, 363–77.

Christian readers. It is fully compatible with the view that in Acts 28:25–28 Luke denounced the Jews collectively and irrevocably.

We have now reviewed the most important arguments that have been raised in favour of the interpretation that Luke did not "write the Jews off," and found none of them compelling. We may therefore now proceed to discuss the purpose of the existence of the two strands of rhetoric that I have identified in Luke's discourse on Christianity and the Jews. As noted, there may be a slight tension between these. One of them, strand (a), makes Luke's work one of the most "Jewish" in the New Testament in the sense that it puts an unusually strong emphasis on the continuity between Judaism and Christianity; the other, strand (b), however, makes it one of the most "un-Jewish" in the sense that it implies that despite its Jewish heritage, Christianity had eventually evolved into a purely gentile affair. Yet both of them are there. Why? Let us discuss the two strands in turn.

Strand (a). In previous research, it was sometimes suggested that the stress on the continuity between Christianity and the Jewish traditions betrayed an attempt on the part of the author to claim for Christianity the status of Judaism as a *religio licita*. It is now widely recognized, however, that the concept of *religio licita* did not actually form a legal category in the Roman world[50] as this position implies; and since it furthermore assumes that Luke's work had served as a formal apology to the Roman authorities, it has now generally been dismissed. Today, many readers instead connect it to his ambition, discussed in the previous section, to establish the non-novelty (and hence, by implication, the virtue) of the Christian faith.[51] This, I believe, is a fruitful course of analysis. We noted above that not everyone in the ancient world acknowledged the Jewish ethnos as particularly old. Tacitus and others regarded it as a relatively recent offshoot of the Egyptian people. Others, however, so Tacitus informs us, traced it back to the days of the deposition of Saturn, while others yet, offered it "a glorious beginning" (*clara ... initia*) by associating it with the Solymi of Homer (*Hist.* 5.2; cf. *Il.* 6.184; *Od.* 5.282). The

50 H. J. Cadbury, "Some Foibles of New Testament Scholarship," *JBR* 26 (1958): 215–16; Maddox, *Purpose of Luke-Acts*, 91–2; Esler, *Community and Gospel*, 211–14.

51 Esler, *Community and Gospel*, 201–19; Mason, *Josephus and the New Testament*, 266–70.

elder Pliny (5.73) similarly suggested that the Essenes had existed for "thousands of ages" (*per seculorum milia*),[52] and obviously from a biblical perspective the antiquity of the Jews was evident. In any case, disputed though it was, Israel's past formed the only avenue through which Christian writers could hope to lay claim to antiquity. Luke's decision to "plant Jesus' life and Christian origins deeply within the soil of Judaism," as Mason has put it, may thus probably be seen as a materialization of his effort to unshackle Christianity from the epithet of newness.[53] In the previous section I noted that Luke's works contain more manifestations of his wish to dissociate Christianity from the concept of newness than just the texts cited there (i.e., Lk. 4:31–37; 22:7–23; Acts 17:22–31). What I had in mind, it will now be clear, was the wealth of passages through which this act of "planting" takes place.

Strand (b). But what about the other constituent of Luke's discourse on the Jews? Why did he portray the Jews as eventually dismissive of the gospel, violently opposed to Jesus and the church, and irrevocably excluded from the possibility of salvation? Various explanations have been offered. Some scholars have proposed that this aspect of Luke's rhetoric should be seen as a reaction to Jewish antagonism toward the church during the author's own lifetime. Some advocates of this view suggest that the church was being physically harassed,[54] whereas others imagine rather milder forms of opposition.[55] Other interpreters have suggested that it should be seen as a response to an identity crisis among gentile Christians, prompted by the experience of missionary failure among the Jews, whose writings and traditions these Christians nevertheless claimed as their own.[56] Neither of these proposals seems fully convincing. One imagines with regard to the latter that by the time of Luke's

52 Cf. Feldman, *Jew and Gentile*, 182.

53 Mason, *Josephus and the New Testament*, 267.

54 G. Schneider, *Verleugnung, Verspottung und Verhör Jesu nach Lukas 22, 54–71: Studien zur lukanischen Darstellung der Passion*, SANT 22 (Munich: Kösel-Verlag, 1969), 194; E. Haenchen, *The Acts of the Apostle: A Commentary* (Philadelphia, PA: Westminster, 1971), 289–90.

55 P. Winter, *On the Trial of Jesus*, SJ 1 (Berlin; New York, N.Y.: De Gruyter, 1974), 170; J. Gager, *The Origins of Anti-Semitism* (New York, N.Y.: Oxford University Press, 1983), 134–59.

56 Maddox, *Purpose of Luke-Acts*, 183–5; Sanders, *Jews in Luke-Acts*, 313–7.

writings most Christians would have come to terms with the church's predominantly (if not everywhere exclusively) gentile composition, particularly if a second century dating is to be assumed. And regarding the former, little in Luke's work suggests that the church of his own time should have been troubled by Jewish hostility. On three occasions in the gospel (11:49; 12:11; 21:12) Jesus admittedly predicts that believers will come to suffer in the future on account of the Jews, but these predictions are all fulfilled in the course of Acts;[57] and in Acts 20:29–30, when Paul somberly warns the Ephesian elders of the dangers of the church to come, Jewish antagonism is conspicuously absent from his list.

It will come as no surprise, I imagine, that just as I perceive strand (a) in Luke's rhetoric on the Jews to serve to support his endeavour to divorce Christianity from the concept of newness, so I understand strand (b) to serve to support his efforts to prove the political innocuousness of the church. To see how this may work, let us cast a glance at how the Jews were generally perceived in the Roman world around the time of the composition of Luke's works.

Throughout the centuries around the birth of Christianity, the Jews attracted considerable attention from non-Jews. Occasionally in the literature from this period we come across voices that express admiration for their nation, particularly for its strict adherence to monotheistic doctrine. The general tone, however, seems to have been one of disdain and suspicion. In itself this is probably unremarkable. Foreign nations were regularly denigrated by ancient authors. The Britons, for instance, were perceived by Roman writers as uncivilized and the Greeks as sloppy and effeminate. And certain accusations that were levelled against the Jews were also hurled at other nationalities.[58] It is hard to avoid the impression, however, that Jews encountered more antagonism than most foreign peoples.

Two characteristics in particular seem to have attracted gentile disparagement: the Jews' customs, which appeared peculiar and even depraved to many outsiders, and their reluctance to socialize and otherwise mix with people of other ethnicities. The latter in particular earned the Jews

57 Cf. Sanders, *Jews in Luke-Acts*, 310.
58 Cf. Feldman, *Jew and Gentile*, 125.

a reputation for misanthropy. As early as around 300 BCE, Hecataeus (ap. Diod. 40.3.4) described the Jewish lifestyle as "somewhat unsocial" (ἀπάνθρωπον) and "hostile to foreigners" (μισόξενον). A couple of centuries later, Lysimachus (ap. Jos. *C. Ap.* 1.309) suggested that Moses had instructed his compatriots to offer only the worst of advice to non-Jews and to overthrow these people's altars and temples. In the first century CE, Apion (ap. Jos. *C. Ap.* 2.121) suggested that the Jews took an oath to never show friendliness to any aliens. Occasionally, the accusations of Jewish misanthropy would take almost the form of satire. According to Josephus (*C. Ap.* 2.91–96), Apion and "others" (possibly Posidonius and Apollonius Molon mentioned in 2.79) had disseminated a story according to which the Syrian King Antiochus Epiphanes had found a Greek man lying in the temple of Jerusalem held captive there and being fattened up to be slaughtered and his entrails consumed at a traditional festival, during which the participants would also swear to always nurture enmity to the Greeks.

Occasionally Roman authors would perceive Jewish misanthropy as a threat to the peace and stability of the realm. In his defence of Flaccus, a former governor of Asia, accused of among other things pocketing contributions meant for the Jerusalem temple, Cicero suggested that it was, although certainly he seems to have believed that Pompey's conquest of Judea in 63 BCE had subdued the Jewish menace for good:

> Every city ... has its own religious observances and we have ours. Even when Jerusalem was still standing and the Jews were at peace with us, the demands of their religion were incompatible with the majesty of our Empire, the dignity of our name and the institutions of our ancestors; and now that the Jewish nation has shown by armed rebellion what are its feelings for our rule, they are even more so; how dear it was to the immortal gods has been shown by the fact that it has been conquered, farmed out to tax collectors and enslaved (*Flac.* 69).[59]

59 Tr. Mason, *Josephus and the New Testament*, 62.

In 38 CE a violent conflict erupted between Jews and non-Jews in the city of Alexandria. And when in 66, some 125 years after Flaccus' defence, the Jewish war broke out, many Romans appear to have construed this as evidence that the Jews were indeed, as Cicero had implied, an innately belligerent nation liable at any moment to disturb and threaten the Roman political order. The fact that Josephus sensed a need to dismantle such an understanding in his *Jewish War* is suggestive of the effects the rebellion had left on their image in the eyes of the Romans.[60]

That these effects were significant should cause us no surprise. Not only from a Jewish, but also from a Roman perspective, the Jewish war had been a major military event. The siege of Jerusalem had lasted a full five months and the military forces required to subdue the revolt had been extraordinary, considerably larger than those deployed to complete the conquest of Britain in 43 CE.[61] The mere scale of the war sufficed to make it stand out in the public imagination. In addition, the war was made subject to an extraordinary degree of celebration by the Flavian dynasty. On Titus' return from Jerusalem, the Flavians performed a spectacular triumphal procession (Jos. *B.J.* 7.123–157)—the only one to have ever been held to celebrate the defeat of a rebellious province. Furthermore, they initiated a substantial commemorative building program, including the Temple of Peace (that housed the sequestered treasures of the Jerusalem temple), two triumphal arches, one of which emphasized the fierceness of the Jews by claiming, incorrectly, that Jerusalem had never been conquered prior to Titus' campaign, and the Colosseum, which had been erected, according to an inscription discovered in the early 1990s, "from the spoils of war." Moreover, the Flavians issued a series of coins that celebrated *Judea Capta* and imposed the *fiscus judaicus* on the Jews, which, humiliatingly, redirected their previous contributions to the temple in Jerusalem to that of Jupiter Capitoline.[62]

60 Note, for instance, Silius Italicus' characterization of the Jews as "the fierce race of Palestine" (*Pun*. 3.605–606); cf. ibid.

61 F. Millar, "Last Year in Jerusalem: Monuments of War in Rome 1," in *Flavius Josephus and Flavian Rome*, ed. J. Edmondson, S. Mason, and J. Rives (Oxford: Oxford University Press, 2005), 101.

62 Cf. G. Alföldy, "Eine Bauinschrift aus dem Colosseum," *ZPE* 109 (1994): 195–226; Mason, *Josephus and the New Testament*, 60–1; Millar, "Last Year in Jerusalem."

It has sometimes been suggested that during Domitian's reign Jewish mores and beliefs should have attracted numerous gentile sympathizers, not least from the propertied classes, despite the Flavians' anti-Jewish policies and propaganda. L. H. Feldman has even suggested that the particular severity with which Domitian apparently collected the *fiscus judaicus* (Suet. *Dom.* 12.2) had been spurred by irritation on his part with the Jews' "success in winning converts, especially at the court."[63] This understanding rests primarily on a passage from Suetonius (*Dom.* 12.2) and two from Dio Cassius (67.14.1–3; 68.1.2), which suggest that during Domitian's rule several individuals, including members of the imperial family, were accused of (and some of them convicted of) adopting Jewish customs. M. Goodman, however, has persuasively cautioned us against this understanding. Both Suetonius and Dio speak about *accusations*, yet particularly "in an oppressive regime" (such as Domitian's is generally taken to have been), "the fact that an accusation has been made does not prove that a crime has been committed."[64] The evidence from the two historians, if reliable, may indicate nothing more than that the "slur of Jewishness" constituted a convenient rhetorical and legal apparatus for vindictive informers and for the emperor himself. The notion, indeed, that proselytizing Jews should have been "successful in official circles in Rome" under the rule of Domitian, as proposed by Feldman,[65] seems implausible. Few Romans, one imagines, would have felt encouraged to follow the practices of a people and engage in the worship of a God whose temple had recently been raided and burnt to the ground. Whatever attraction "the Jewish way of life" may previously have held for "open-minded" Romans is likely to have abated after 70 CE.[66]

It is possible that pressure on the Jews diminished with Nerva's ascension to the throne. Again, however, we should proceed with interpretive care. Coins issued during his reign boast that he put an end to "the malicious accusations" that had been connected with the *fiscus judaicus*

63 Feldman, *Jew and Gentile*, 100.

64 M. Goodman, "The *Fiscus Iudaicus* and Gentile Attitudes to Judaism in Flavian Rome," in *Flavius Josephus and Flavian Rome*, ed. J. Edmondson, S. Mason, and J. Rives (Oxford: Oxford University Press, 2005), 167–79, esp. 174.

65 Feldman, *Jew and Gentile*, 332.

66 Goodman, "*Fiscus Iudaicus*," 173–4.

(*Fisci Iudaici Calumnia Sublati*) and Dio (68.1.2) reports that he prohibited accusations of a Jewish mode of life. This may indicate that he took a more lenient attitude toward Jews than his predecessor had done, but it could also signal merely that he had brought an end to the golden age of the informers, who had apparently flourished under Domitian and availed themselves of such charges.

However we interpret the evidence relating to Nerva's reign (96–98), anti-Jewish sentiment appears to have blossomed under his *filius adoptivus* Trajan (98–117). The *fiscus judaicus* remained in force and Trajan is reported to have taken exceptional offence at one point when a lawyer representing a group of Alexandrians insinuated that his clients could not expect to receive a fair hearing, since the emperor was under the influence of the *consilium principii*, several members of which, he claimed, were "impious" Jews (*P. Oxy.* 1242). What roused the emperor's anger was hardly the attorney's depreciatory description of the Jews, but rather his claim that he should have been under the sway of Jews, which certainly was not correct. As J. Bennett has noted, at most one member of Trajan's *consilium* can be identified with Jewish roots (a certain T. Julius Alexander Julianus, who may or may not have been the son of Philo of Alexandria's nephew, T. Julius Alexander, who had served, however, as a general in Judea beside Vespasian, as Trajan's own father, M. Ulpius Traianus, had done).[67] Anti-Jewish temperament is visible in the literature from the period as well. And interestingly for our purposes, writers of this age would continue the line from Cicero and hint at an inherent disposition for revolt and violent opposition in the Jews. In the autumn of Domitian's reign, Quintilian (3.7.21) had pointed to Moses to illustrate his claim that "it is a disgrace to founders of cities to gather together a race pernicious to everybody else" (tr. Russell, LCL).[68] And during Trajan's rule, Tacitus, whom we noted earlier to have ascribed several possible origins to the Jews, most of which were uncomplimentary, claimed that the Jews nurture a "hostile hatred toward all others" (*adversus omnis alios hostile odium*) and induce those who adopt their customs to disown their own country (*Hist.* 5.5; cf. also Juv. *Sat.*

67 J. Bennett, *Trajan:* Optimus Princeps*: A Life and Times* (Bloomington, IN: Indiana University Press, 1997), 105.

68 Feldman, *Jew and Gentile*, 129.

14.103–104). In 116, in the East (Cyrene), violent clashes erupted once again between Jews and non-Jews. Our Roman source for the events, Dio Cassius 68.32, predictably blames the Jews and mentions the perpetration of appalling atrocities. Whatever the historical credibility of his account, his rhetoric appears to presume an anti-Jewish disposition on the part of his audience and it is hard to avoid the impression that Philostratus (*Apol.* 5.33) must have spoken for many when much later, in the early third century, he ruminated through one of his characters (the Stoic philosopher Euphrates) that perhaps it would have been better if Judea had never been annexed.[69]

In the first section of this chapter we noted three reasons why in the Roman world Christians might sometimes not have been perceived as politically harmless. To these we may now add a fourth. The sources visited above justify the assessment that during the centuries around the birth of Christianity the Jewish nation figured in the imagination of the Roman public as a people susceptible to violent rebellion and disturbance of the civic order. Given that the members of the Christian movement worshipped the Jewish God and regarded themselves as heirs to the Jewish traditions, it might have seemed natural for many to assume that the Christians were in some sense themselves Jewish and hence likely in a similar fashion to form a threat to the political order and peace and stability of the empire.

Given his ambition to prove the innocuousness of the church, it is clear that Luke needed, in one way or another, to preempt or contravene this possible line of reasoning. He could have done so, of course, by seeking to disprove the Roman prejudice of the Jews as a particularly riotous people, much like Josephus (cf., e.g., *B.J.* 2.450, 390–395; 4.97; 5.335, 547), and thereby attempt to implicitly exonerate the Christians, too. Instead, however, he chose to pursue a different strategy, namely to (i) confirm the Roman stereotype of the Jews and then (ii) forcefully contrast them with the church. We have already seen how he did this, but let us elaborate.

Luke confirms the Roman stereotype of the Jews in a number of ways. In the gospel, for instance, he portrays them as demanding the release

69 Cf. ibid.; Bennett, *Trajan:* Optimus Princeps, 201.

of a man "who had been thrown into prison for insurrection (στάσιν) ... and murder (φόνον)" (23:18–19)[70] and as executing Jesus by mob lynching (23:26–38). Likewise, in Acts, he claims that they stoned Stephen (7:57–59) and on several occasions attacked the missionaries in the public arena and incited the crowds to violent conduct (13:50; 14:1–5; 17:5–9, 13; 21:27; 22:22). In one case he even suggests that they assaulted a fellow Jew in front of the governor's tribunal (18:17). Luke, to be sure, did not ascribe riotous conduct solely to the Jews (cf. Acts 14:1–5; 16:19–24; 19:21–40). Like Roman writers, Luke was aware, and happy to report, that civil unrest was a common phenomenon, not exclusive to any one nationality. But also like Roman writers, he nevertheless portrayed the Jewish people as particularly unruly. Readers biased by Roman prejudice can only be expected to have nodded with a sense of recognition at Luke's portrayal of the Jews.

Luke encourages his readers to contrast the Christians with the Jews in three different ways. First, in the latter parts of his works he depicts the Jews as generally hostile to the church. By so doing, he invites his readers to conceptualize the relationship between the Christians and the Jews as one of difference rather than similarity. Second, whenever he represents the Jews as belligerent or riotous, he consistently portrays Jesus and/or the missionaries as either the innocent victims of their aggression or, alternatively, as peaceful bystanders to it. I noted above that it was probably important for Luke to clarify that the Christians had in no way been responsible for the rejection and hostility to which they were exposed from the side of the Jews, and I may now clarify why. If the Christians could in some sense have been seen as having incited the antagonism of the Jews, the contrast between the Jews and the Christians would have seemed less unambiguous, and it could have been difficult to perceive the Jews as solely accountable for the violence that accompanied the "parting of the ways." As it is, however, it is clear that whatever violent conflict occurred during the years of the early mission was a result of entirely unwarranted Jewish aggression. Third, in Acts 28:25–28, as we have seen, Luke "writes the Jews

70 Cf. Conzelmann (*Theology of St. Luke*, 140), "xxiii, 18 ff. underline [the Jews'] solidarity with the political insurgent—in contrast with Mark."

off." By so doing he clarifies that the church of the postapostolic era, including his own time, was and forever would remain an entirely gentile association. In sum, in these three ways Luke clarified for his readers that whatever might be said to characterize the church, it was certainly an exclusively non-Jewish society. And that, among other things (cf. above), could be taken to prove its political legitimacy.

We have now seen that strand (a) of Luke's discourse on Christianity and the Jews may be seen to have served to liberate the church from the epithet of newness and strand (b) to verify its political innocence. Without further ado, we may therefore conclude that, like the material examined in the previous two sections, this discourse, too, may be taken to have been shaped by Luke with a view to recasting Christianity in a way that he thought would make it appear more palatable to Theophilus.

I have now analysed Luke's discourse on "Christianity and Rome," "Christianity and novelty," and Christianity and the Jews," and shown how this discourse is compatible with the theory outlined in chapter 1 about Luke and Theophilus. In the following two chapters I will turn first to his discourse on possessions and then to his discourse on the family.

3
Luke and Possessions

In the early chapters of Acts, Luke explains that the members of the first Christian congregation in Jerusalem practised what scholars have generally agreed to call "a community of goods." "The whole group of those who believed," he informs us, "were of one heart and soul, and no one claimed private ownership of any possessions." On the contrary, "everything they owned was held in common" (4:32). In practical terms, what these early Christians did was to sell whatever property they had and hand over the proceeds to the apostles, who would then distribute them within the community in accordance with everyone's needs (4:34–37). According to Luke, this early period of the church was an idyllic time. The community, as noted in the previous chapter, was greatly esteemed by "the people," i.e., by the non-Christian Jews (2:47; cf. 4:33), and the fact that all members renounced their possessions for the sake of the common good meant that no one among them was poor or needy, οὐδὲ γὰρ ἐνδεής τις ἦν ἐν αὐτοῖς (4:34).

However, as also noted, the idyll did not last. Tensions with the people and its leaders soon developed. Already in 4:3 Peter and John had been arrested and forced to defend themselves before the Jerusalem notables (4:5–22). In 5:18 the apostles were detained. In 6:8–7:60 Stephen was brought before the Jerusalem council and stoned to death. And in 8:1 a Jewish persecution of the church broke out, on account of which all of its members, except the apostles, fled and were scattered all over Judea and Samaria. This spelt the end of the first congregation. It also spelt the end of the community of goods that it had practised. Although we later hear of a new congregation in Jerusalem (21:20), neither this nor any other church of which Luke speaks reinstated this type of communal organization. Similarly, we do not hear of anyone relinquishing all their possessions ever again.

Yet even before the congregation had been physically disbanded through external pressure, cracks in its unity and commitment to sharing had started to emerge. In 5:1–11 we read the story of Ananias and Sapphira, who only surrendered some of their possessions to the community, keeping some back for their own private use. They were immediately afterwards struck dead at Peter's feet on hearing his words of condemnation. And in 6:1 we learn of a dispute between the Hebrews and the Hellenists on account of the widows of the latter being neglected in the daily distribution. Interestingly, although Luke connects the outbreak of this strife, temporally at least, to the expansion of this nascent church, he does not seem to imply that it resulted from any dearth of resources. In 6:2–7 he presumes and proves that if only a team of specialized deacons could be assigned to the supervision of the tables, then the food available to the community would be adequate to satisfy all. Apparently, then, the experience of need and poverty had been the outcome for some of a sense of disunity in the church, rather than the other way around.

Why did Luke ascribe to the first Christians a community of goods; why did he suggest that it was never restored again after the dissolution of the first congregation; and why did he allow it to show signs of weakness prior to the persecutions of 8:1? We will return to these questions at the end of the chapter.

In this chapter we examine Luke's ethics of possessions. This subject has long been recognized as an exegetical conundrum. The trouble is that although the topic of possessions seems to have been important to Luke, his teaching on how to relate to them appears contradictory. Some forty years ago, L. T. Johnson remarked, with good reason, that "although Luke consistently talks about possessions, he does not talk about possessions consistently."[1] Much prior research on Luke has sought to demon-

1 L. T. Johnson, *The Literary Function of Possessions in Luke-Acts*, SBLDS 39 (Missoula, MT: Scholars Press, 1977), 233. Some interpreters discuss Luke's wealth ethics, however, without noticing any contradictions (see, e.g., Esler, *Community and Gospel*, 164–200; O. Lehtipuu "The Rich, the Poor, and the Promise of an Eschatological Reward in the Gospel of Luke," in *Other Worlds and Their Relation to This World*, ed.

strate, however, that the inconsistencies are only apparent and that once his writings are subjected to proper hermeneutical scrutiny, they will emerge as conveying a fully coherent ethical vision. I disagree with that view. I certainly believe that scholars have sometimes exaggerated the number of incongruities in Luke's works. For instance, unlike many interpreters I do not perceive a contradiction between Luke's imperatives concerning almsgiving (Lk. 6:27–36; 11:41) and the divestiture of possessions (Lk. 12:33; 14:33; 18:22), and unlike several others I also believe that his portrayal in the early chapters of Acts of the first congregation, with its emphasis on its community of sharing, reflects the same ethical stance as the one that governs the rest of his second volume. But there are, in my view, a number of inconsistencies that cannot be dissolved and must be considered as "real." As we shall see, some of these are internal to Luke's gospel, but arguably the most important line of incongruity is to be found between the gospel and Acts. My purpose in this chapter is to clarify the nature of these contradictions and offer a plausible explanation as to why they exist.

I shall begin by offering an overview of Luke's teaching on possessions in the gospel and Acts, respectively. Since literature on this topic abounds,[2] I shall keep the overview brief and bring in other interpreters mainly when the readings that I propose are likely to seem contro-

T. Nicklas, J. Verheyden, and M. M. Eynikel, Supplement to the Journal for the Study of Judaism 143 [Leiden; Boston, MS: Brill, 2010], 229–46).

2 Important monographs include H.-J. Degenhardt, *Lukas, Evangelist der Armen: Besitz und Besitzverzicht in den Lukanischen Schriften: Eine traditions- und redaktionsgeschichtliche Untersuchung* (Stuttgart: Verlag Kath. Bibelwerk, 1965); Johnson, *Literary Function of Possessions*; D. P. Seccombe, *Possessions and the Poor in Luke-Acts*, SNTSU, B 6 (Linz: A. Fuchs, 1982); F. W. Horn, *Glaube und Handeln in der Theologie des Lukas*, GTA 26 (Göttingen: Vandenhoeck & Ruprecht, 1983); L. Schottroff and W. Stegemann, *Jesus von Nazareth: Hoffnung der Armen* (Stuttgart: W. Kohlhammer, 1990); K. Mineshige, *Besitzverzicht und Almosengeben: Wesen und Forderung des lukanischen Vermögensethos*, WUNT 2.163 (Tübingen: Mohr Siebeck, 2003); V. Petracca, *Gott oder das Geld: Die Besitzethik des Lukas*, Texte und Arbeiten zum neutestamentlichen Zeitalter 39 (Tübingen: Francke, 2003); H.-G. Gradl, *Zwischen Arm und Reich: Das lukanische Doppelwerk in leserorientierter und textpragmatischer Perspektive*, FB 107 (Würzburg: Echter, 2005); J. A. Metzger, *Consumption and Wealth in Luke's Travel Narrative*, Biblical Interpretation Series 88 (Leiden; Boston, MS: Brill, 2007); and C. M. Hays, *Luke's Wealth Ethics: A Study in Their Coherence and Character*, WUNT 2.275 (Tübingen: Mohr Siebeck, 2010).

versial. My aim will be to emphasize the heterogeneity of Luke's teaching both in the gospel itself and between the gospel and Acts. In this section I shall allow myself to bracket out Luke's description of the first congregation in Jerusalem as we will return to this at the end of the chapter. Afterwards I shall turn to the history of research and discuss the ways in which scholars have variously tried to dissolve the inconsistencies in Luke's teaching. I shall argue that none of the attempts that have been made are satisfactory and suggest that we should therefore content ourselves with the notion that the contradictions are genuine and inexorable. Then, on the basis of this suggestion, I shall proceed to offer an explanation as to why they exist. In that section I shall draw and slightly expand on my theory about Luke and Theophilus as presented in chapter 1. And finally in the last section I shall return to Luke's description of the first congregation and answer the questions raised above and consider how this description may be seen to cohere with and support the perception of Luke's treatment of possessions that by then will have been developed.

Luke's Teaching on Possessions

Let us begin by surveying Luke's gospel and then afterwards proceed to Acts.

As noted, the teachings on wealth in Luke's gospel are not free from contradiction. Nevertheless, I propose that the majority of its passages dealing with possessions may be seen as, together, conveying a single ethical code. This code can be summarized as follows: the possession of wealth is incompatible with salvation, and to render themselves worthy of redemption believers must renounce their possessions for the benefit of the poor and adopt a very modest standard of living, and even after having done so continue to offer charity to those in need. We begin our survey by examining those texts that, together, articulate this paradigm and afterwards turn to the passages that deviate from it.

The notion that wealth is irreconcilable with salvation emerges from a number of texts in Luke's gospel. Apart from the "woes to the rich" in 6:24–26, which, given the contrast with 6:20–23, appears to exclude the rich from the prospect of redemption, and the presumably prophetic announcement by Mary in 1:52–53 (her use of the aorist form, notwithstanding),[3] three passages in particular emphasize this. These are the parable of the rich fool (12:16–21), the parable of the rich man and Lazarus (16:19–31), and the story of Jesus' encounter with the rich ruler (18:18–30). Let us discuss each of these in turn, starting with the last.

We touched upon Luke 18:18–30 briefly in chapter 1. The pericope features a dialogue between Jesus and a rich ἄρχων—probably to be understood as a member of the Jewish council (the Sanhedrin) or a leader of a synagogue or of one of the Jewish parties[4]—and a subsequent conversation between Jesus and his followers. As will be recalled, the ruler asks Jesus what it will take for him to inherit eternal life. There is no doubt, of course, that the notion of eternal life operates as a synonym for salvation. After a brief exchange about the man's record of commitment to the Decalogue, Jesus informs him that he will need to sell all (πάντα) his belongings, distribute the proceeds among the poor, and register as a disciple (18:22). At this, the ruler despairs.

The fact that Jesus' response sets up a contrast between holding on to wealth and attaining eternal life—or as he puts it "treasure in heaven" (18:22), again a synonym for salvation—suggests that the passage identifies wealth and the attainment of salvation as mutually exclusive, which is what I have proposed to be the general position of Luke's gospel.[5] A number of scholars, however, opt for less rigorous interpretations. According to one line of exegesis, Jesus' instruction in 18:22 should be seen as relevant, and normative only for the ruler, not for rich people in general. Jesus, on this view, should have recognized that this particular man was so attached to his wealth that for him to engage in service to God (of any acceptable kind) would be impracticable without an initial act of divestiture. Unless he were to renounce his wealth before committing himself to such service, he would end up feeling torn between

3 Cf. F. Bovon, *Lk. 1: A Commentary on the Gospel of Lk. 1:1–9:50*, Hermeneia (Minneapolis, MN: Fortress Press, 2002), 62–3; Wolter, *Lukasevangelium*, 104.

4 Cf., e.g., Tannehill, *Narrative Unity: Luke*, 187.

5 Cf. also Cassidy, *Jesus, Politics and Society*, 26–7; Metzger, *Consumption and Wealth*, 165.

mammon and his allegiance to God (cf. 16:13). The passage should thus be seen to leave other rich people who are less obsessed with belongings free to hold on to their property, and to do so without needing to fear for their eschatological fate.[6]

In my assessment, this reading is problematic for two reasons. First, Luke nowhere suggests that the ruler should be seen as "a special case," as this reading requires.[7] Second, the ensuing dialogue between Jesus and the disciples clearly indicates that Jesus intended to identify wealth as an impediment to salvation in itself (irrespective of one's level of attachment to it), and hence his instruction in 18:22 as applicable to all rich people. Thus, in 18:25 he famously notes, in explicitly general terms, that "it is easier for a camel to go through the eye of a needle than for *someone who is rich* to enter the kingdom of God."

Another line of analysis accepts that Jesus' commandment in 18:22 should be seen as pertinent to all rich people, but contends that his further comment in 18:27 alleviates the severity of its message, as well as that of 18:25. In 18:26, in reaction to his stern declaration in 18:25, Jesus' followers ask him "who" then "will be able to be saved?" (τίς δύναται σωθῆναι). And Jesus responds, "What is impossible for humans is possible for God" (τὰ ἀδύνατα παρὰ ἀνθρώποις δυνατὰ παρὰ τῷ θεῷ ἐστιν) (18:27). According to the advocates of this second line of interpretation, 18:27 should be seen as establishing a loophole for the rich. What Jesus meant to imply was that even if the rich fail to comply with the instruction of 18:22, and accordingly ought to be excluded from the Kingdom in keeping with the teaching of 18:25, God might choose to show mercy on them and offer them salvation nonetheless. In that way, it is proposed, 18:27 offers "eine Relativierung von V. 25, die auch den

6 Seccombe, *Possessions and the Poor,* 126–7; D. J. Ireland, *Stewardship and the Kingdom of God: An Historical, Exegetical, and Contextual Study of the Parable of the Unjust Steward in Lk. 16:1–13,* SNT 70 (Leiden: Brill, 1992), 186–7; T. E. Phillips, *Reading Issues of Wealth and Poverty in Luke-Acts,* Studies in Bible and Early Christianity 48 (Lewiston, N.Y.: E. Mellen Press, 2001), 163–4, the latter cited in Metzger, *Consumption and Wealth,* 165.

7 Seccombe (*Possessions and the Poor,* 126) recognizes this; cf. also Hays, *Luke's Wealth Ethics,* 172–3.

Reichen Hoffnung gibt."[8] Strictly speaking, then, the rich are unworthy of salvation, and in that sense "incapable" of it, but God, being God, is capable of everything, and may therefore in the end redeem them all the same.

This understanding would be convincing were it not for the fact that Peter's conversation with Jesus in the following verses suggests that even after the latter's comment in 18:27, both of them continue to think of divestiture as a soteriological requirement. Thus, in 18:28 Peter points to the fact that he and the other disciples have all left τὰ ἴδια for the sake of following Jesus, and thus acted in accordance with the commandment of 18:22; and in 18:29–30 Jesus responds that neither they nor anyone else who acts in a similar way will fail to obtain a reward, in this life or the next, for the sacrifices they have made. In this light, I believe, it is preferable, with scholars such as Marshall, Green, and Metzger, to perceive Jesus in 18:27 as pointing not to an ability in God to redeem the rich in spite of any failure on their part to renounce their wealth, but to an ability in God to instill in the minds of the rich a willingness to renounce, and hence a capacity in them to be saved by complying with the commandment of 18:22.[9] As Metzger explains, Peter's question in 18:26 should probably be seen as an attempt to emphasize the "nearly insurmountable hurdle" for the rich "in divesting" themselves of their affluence (given the power that possessions typically exert on humans), and Jesus' response in the following verse as an expression of agreement with his disciple on this point and a clarification that God's assistance in this is and always will be required.[10]

Luke's story of Jesus and the rich ruler thus identifies wealth and salvation as categorically incompatible. By choosing wealth one simultaneously chooses to opt out of the prospect of salvation. The same message, I propose, emerges from the parable of the rich man and Lazarus. This parable features a rich unnamed individual (occasionally referred to as Dives in the scholarly literature, on the basis of the Latin word for "rich"

8 Wolter, *Lukasevangelium*, 601; cf. also Fitzmyer, *Luke X–XXIV*, 1203; Hays, *Luke's Wealth Ethics*, 171; F. Bovon, *Lk. 2: A Commentary on the Gospel of Lk. 9:51–19:27*, Hermeneia (Minneapolis, MN: Fortress Press, 2013), 568.

9 Marshall, *Luke*, 686; Green, *Luke*, 657–8; Metzger, *Consumption and Wealth*, 168.

10 Ibid.

applied in the Vulgate; cf. 16:19), who lives in extreme luxury, and a beggar by the name of Lazarus, who lay at his gate "covered with sores" longing "to be satisfied with what fell from the rich man's table" (16:20–21). One day Lazarus dies, and soon after the rich man follows. But whereas Lazarus is carried by angels, upon his death, into the realm of heaven, "into Abraham's bosom" (16:22), the rich man is despatched into the flames of hell, where he is exposed to excruciating suffering. Once he wakes up there, he sees Abraham and Lazarus from afar and begs the former to send Lazarus "to dip the tip of his finger in water and cool [his] tongue" to soothe his pain. Abraham flatly denies the request (however modest it may seem). For one thing, he explains, granting this wish would be impossible as hell and heaven are separated by "a great chasm" (χάσμα μέγα), which effectively prevents any passage between the two. But more importantly, the rich man should recognize that his sufferings now in the depths of "Tartarus" are justified, since, as the patriarch puts it, he had already received his "good things" (ἀγαθά) while he was alive, whereas Lazarus, who is comforted now in heaven, had only received "evil things" (κακά) (16:25–26).

Abraham's answer suggests a strikingly mechanistic perspective, according to which the rich man, and by implication affluent people generally, are automatically consigned to anguish in the afterlife simply on account of their wealth. Affluence in this life inevitably leads to suffering in the next one.[11] This, indeed, is the lesson that I take the parable to teach. As with the story of Jesus and the rich ruler, however, several observers have suggested that Luke did not intend quite such a radical message.[12] These interpreters typically accept that if taken by itself Abraham's response to the rich man in 16:25 would suggest such a view, but contend that the import of that answer should be assessed in the light of 16:27–31, which continues the dialogue between Abraham and

11 Cf. also R. Bauckham, "The Rich Man and Lazarus: The Parable and the Parallels," *NTS* 37, no. 2 (1991): 232–3; Evans, *Saint Luke*, 611–16; Metzger, *Consumption and Wealth*, 146; H. Roose, "Umkehr und Ausgleich bei Lukas: Die Gleichnisse vom verlorenen Sohn (Lk 15.11–32) und vom reichen Mann und armen Lazarus (Lk 16.19–31) als Schwestergeschichten," *NTS* 56, no. 1 (2010): 8–10.

12 E.g., Tannehill, *Narrative Unity: Luke*, 131–2; Wolter, *Lukasevangelium*, 562–3; Hays, *Luke's Wealth Ethics*, 156–8; Bovon, *Lk*. 2, 481; cf. also Degenhardt, *Evangelist der Armen*, 133–5; Green, *Luke*, 308–10; Kim, *Stewardship and Almsgiving*, 213–14.

"Dives." In response to the rejection of his first request, the rich man rejoins:

> "Then, father, I ask you to send him to my father's house for I have five brothers that he may warn them, so that they will not also come into this place of torment." Abraham replied, "They have Moses and the prophets; they should listen to them." He said, "No, father Abraham; but if someone goes to them from the dead, they will repent." He said to him, "If they do not listen to Moses and the prophets, neither will they be convinced even if someone rises from the dead."

In this second request the rich man changes his focus from his own fate to that of his (presumably similarly rich) brothers. His petition suggests that if these were warned by his example through the intervention of Lazarus, they would be able to reform their lives in a way that would lead them to salvation rather than damnation (where otherwise they seem to be heading). If, as I and others have argued, Luke intended through this parable to signal that wealth and salvation were mutually incompatible, this implies that the only course of action available to the five, if they wanted to avoid their brother's fate, was to divest themselves of their wealth. Only by ceasing to be rich would they be able to avoid the flames of hell. This, then, is what the rich man should be seen as imploring Abraham to bring Lazarus to inform them. Yet according to the interpreters cited above, Abraham's comments in 18:29 and 18:31 about "Moses and the prophets" demonstrate that divestiture of wealth was not what Luke had in mind. For in those comments Abraham implies that the type of information that Lazarus would give the brothers, if indeed he were dispatched to them, was already available to them in the Mosaic and prophetic literature. And neither the Pentateuch nor the books of the prophets anywhere condemn the possession of wealth or encourages the rich to divest themselves of their property. On the contrary, they repeatedly stipulate sharing and the offering of charity. Hence, they suggest, Abraham should be seen in that verse as implying that the brothers of the rich man could remain rich and still escape the torments of hell if only, in keeping with the scriptural prescripts, they would begin to act generously toward those in need. And when seen in that light, it becomes clear that the rich man himself was not condemned because he was rich, but rather, in the words of Hays, because he had neglected the Torah insofar as he had failed "to extend food, clothing, and alms to Lazarus, who [was] starving, naked, and impoverished" (de-italicized).[13] When taken as a whole, it thus emerges that the passage establishes as an obstacle to salvation not the possession of affluence as such, but rather the failure of (some) affluent people to use parts of their wealth to provide for the poor.

This construction is hardly sustainable, however, as in the end it does not interpret 16:25 in the light of 16:27–31 as much as it allows the former of these texts to eclipse the latter. Surely, what is required is a reading of the parable that is able to make sense of the passage as a whole and perceive the two texts as mutually compatible. Yet none of the scholars cited above demonstrates how 16:25 may be seen to cohere with the construction that they ascribe to 16:27–31, and I fail to see how that can be done. That verse, as far as I can see, squarely rules out any possibility of a salvation for the rich (if, that is, they remain rich), and says nothing about charity. Fortunately, however, we do not need to interpret 16:27–31 in the manner proposed by these commentators. It is true, of course, that neither Moses nor the prophets condemn wealth or stipulate a divestiture of possessions. But that hardly requires us to conclude that Luke did not understand them to have done so. In the previous chapter we noted that Luke perceived the life of Jesus and the history of the early church to have developed in strict accordance with scriptural prediction. That by itself should be enough to caution us against thinking that Luke took away from the biblical texts only what was actually there. And we know for a fact that he occasionally perceived in the biblical literature things that it manifestly did not contain (cf., e.g., Lk. 16:17–18). I thus consider it quite plausible that Luke could have understood both "Moses and the prophets" to have condemned the possession of wealth and demanded of the rich that they divest themselves of their affluence, although as modern critical readers we may certainly choose to differ. In sum, the most satisfactory understanding of the parable—satisfactory in the sense that it leaves none of its parts unaccounted for—is that Luke

13 Hays, *Luke's Wealth Ethics*, 158.

did in fact intend it to convey that wealth was incompatible with salvation and, unless forsaken (for instance, in the manner described in 18:22), conducive to damnation.

In 12:13 "someone in the crowd" asks Jesus to instruct his brother to divide the family inheritance with him (εἰπὲ τῷ ἀδελφῷ μου μερίσασθαι μετ' ἐμοῦ τὴν κληρονομίαν). The nature of the man's request is ambiguous. According to Deuteronomy 21:17, the eldest son of the family was entitled to a "double portion" (διπλᾶ) of his father's inheritance (cf. also Num. 27:1–11; 36:7–9). The man of Luke 12:13, presumably the younger of two brothers, may thus be seen as either disputing the fairness of this law and wishing for Jesus to secure him an equal share with his brother; or he may be seen as appealing to the law in a situation where the elder brother had claimed the whole of the inheritance for himself.[14] Other scenarios may also be possible. Whatever the case (Luke intriguingly shows little interest in clarifying the matter), Jesus unambiguously declines the petition, "'Man, who set me to be a judge or arbitrator over you?' And he said to them, 'Take care! Be on your guard against all kinds of greed; for one's life does not consist in the abundance of possessions'" (12:14–15). In 12:16–21 he elaborates on this rejection by offering them the "parable of the rich fool." This parable features a rich farmer (cf. ἀνθρώπου τινὸς πλουσίου) whose lands had yielded abundantly. In response to this he decides to tear down his old barns and erect some larger ones in which he will be able to store his produce and other goods, while musing that by so doing he will secure for himself the means to live joyfully and lavishly for many years to come. Immediately afterwards, however, God intervenes and rebukes him for his thoughts (ἄφρων) and conveys to him that he will die that very night. In conclusion, Jesus (or the Lucan narrator) observes that "So it is with any who stores up treasures for himself and is not rich toward God" (οὕτως ὁ θησαυρίζων ἑαυτῷ καὶ μὴ εἰς θεὸν πλουτῶν) (12:21).

What message was Luke trying to get across through this parable? Few doubt that he portrays the announcement by God of the man's imminent death in 12:20 as a form of punishment for his behaviour, and indeed as

14 Metzger, *Consumption and Wealth*, 65.

a sort of foreshadowing of his eschatological doom.[15] And clearly, he was portraying the conduct of the farmer as an example of what not to do. But exactly what was it about his comportment that Luke found so reprehensible, and depicted as worthy of heavenly damnation? Some interpreters propose that Luke was not so much concerned with the man's ambition to "store up treasures" for himself as he was with his evident lack of concern for those less fortunate than himself. This understanding takes the καὶ μή of 12:21 to imply that it is possible to combine "storing up treasures" for oneself with "being rich toward God," but suggests that the latter of these implies caring for the poor in the sense of providing for their needs, and that this is precisely what the farmer had not been doing (or had any intention of doing in the future). Green, for instance, an advocate of this position, remarks that the parable denounces not "simply those with possessions, but more particularly those whose dispositions are not toward the needs of those around them."[16] Similarly, K. Mineshige writes that "Der Reiche wird nur deshalb verurteilt, weil er sein vermögen ausschließlich für sich selbst verwendet hat."[17] According to this understanding, then, the farmer would have been justified in pursuing the attainment of wealth if at the same time he would also have allowed the needy to share in it. In consequence, the exhortative thrust of the parable emerges as a summons to the rich to give alms and thereby supply for "the needs of the poor."[18]

Two factors, however, militate against this view and suggest that Luke intended the parable to convey largely the same message as the one I have ascribed to the two passages analysed above. Both of these factors have to do with the context of the story. First, Jesus' paraenetic application of the parable in 12:22–34 shows that he was not merely intending to encourage the rich to give alms. Thus, in 12:33b he urges his listeners to "make purses for [themselves] that do not wear out," but constitute "an unfailing treasure in heaven." Clearly, as Wolter has noted, possessing "unfailing treasure in heaven" corresponds to being "rich toward God."[19]

15 Cf., e.g., Seccombe, *Possessions and the Poor*, 143; Hays, *Luke's Wealth Ethics*, 127.
16 Green, *Luke*, 491.
17 Mineshige, *Besitzverzicht und Almosengeben*, 129–30.
18 Hays, *Luke's Wealth Ethics*, 127; cf. Kim, *Stewardship and Almsgiving*, 181–4.
19 Wolter, *Lukasevangelium*, 450–1.

Yet in 12:33a Jesus indicates that obtaining such treasure takes more than a simple extension of charity. It requires, in fact, a "selling," i.e., a divestiture, of one's possessions for the benefit of the poor (πωλήσατε τὰ ὑπάρχοντα ὑμῶν καὶ δότε ἐλεημοσύνην). This suggests that the καὶ μή of 12:21 denotes an "opposition of necessity" between the alternatives listed: one cannot be rich toward God and at the same time store up treasures for oneself.[20] On the contrary, obtaining such richness requires a movement in the exact opposite direction. Luke 12:22–31 coheres with that reading. For in these verses Jesus exhorts his listeners, precisely against the background of the story of the rich farmer (cf. διὰ τοῦτο λέγω ὑμῖν) (12:22), to be unconcerned about how to obtain the necessities of life (something that hardly combines easily with storing up treasure for oneself). Second, as noted in the above, in its own narrative context the parable serves to explain why Jesus declined the request of the speaker of 12:13. Yet certainly, if the point of the parable was merely to encourage the rich to give alms, it would serve that purpose poorly, for that request, as will be recalled, had nothing to do with the topic of almsgiving. By contrast, if, as I suggest, the point of the parable was to encourage the listeners, and the readers of Luke, to avoid the possession of wealth altogether, along the lines of 16:19–31 and 18:18–34, it serves its purpose excellently. For clearly, obtaining wealth (however, precisely, his petition should be construed) was exactly what the man of 12:13 was attempting to do through his appeal to Jesus.

So to return to our earlier question, what was it about the behaviour of the farmer that Luke found so reprehensible and worthy of God's anger? The answer is that he stored up treasures for himself. By no means, he implies, should wealth be pursued (the way it had been by both the petitioner of 12:13 and the farmer); and if it has been obtained (even in moderate proportions; see further below), it must be relinquished for the benefit of the poor (12:33). Failing to comply with that renders one liable to heavenly judgment.

The texts analysed above suggest that the possession of wealth and salvation are fundamentally incompatible. They do not, however, suggest that the rich are categorically beyond the possibility of redemp-

20 Cf. Johnson, *Luke*, 199.

tion. Quite the opposite, Jesus' reply in 18:22 to the rich ruler reveals that there was a way for him to become worthy of "eternal life." And the exchange in 16:27–31 between Abraham and "the rich man" presumes that the fates of the latter's (apparently rich) brothers were not as yet sealed, and that they might obtain deliverance if only they would listen to Moses and the prophets. But they do suggest that in order for them to do so, and avoid heavenly judgment, they must renounce their property. The rich, to put things differently, are capable of salvation, but not if they choose to remain rich.

Luke's gospel, however, does not identify divestiture of possessions as a soteriological requirement for the rich alone. In 12:33, one of the texts cited above, Jesus issues his commandment to "sell your possessions" indiscriminately to the crowd, not aiming his message specifically at the rich. And in 14:33, once more addressing a sizeable group, undoubtedly including at least some people of relatively humble means, he declares that "none of you can become my disciple if you do not relinquish all of your possessions" (πᾶς ἐξ ὑμῶν ὃς οὐκ ἀποτάσσεται πᾶσιν τοῖς ἑαυτοῦ ὑπάρχουσιν οὐ δύναται εἶναί μου μαθητής). And lest anyone should be unsure about the consequences of disobeying that instruction, he adds the following warning, metaphorically describing the disciples as salt, "Salt is good; but if salt becomes tasteless, how will it become salty again? It is fit neither for the soil nor for the manure pile; they throw it away (ἔξω βάλλουσιν αὐτό). Let anyone with ears to hear listen" (ὁ ἔχων ὦτα ἀκούειν ἀκουέτω) (14:34–35).

The reading that I propose here of 14:33–35 presumes that Luke regarded discipleship as a precondition for salvation. I should note that not everyone agrees with that view. It is occasionally suggested that Luke should have perceived discipleship as only one of two (or possibly more) viable responses to the εὐαγγέλιον, both (or all) of which may potentially lead to redemption. Discipleship, on this view, constitutes a particularly fervent form of commitment to Christ, which not everyone was, or is, required to assume. If that is true, then surely the directive about divestiture of possessions in 14:33 (and possibly also in 12:33) as well as the menace of 14:34–35 should be seen as aimed not at believers in general, but only at those particular individuals who had registered for the extremely dedicated service to Christ that discipleship involves, in addition, of course, to any who might contemplate doing so. This view is associated primarily with what Hays has identified as the bi-vocational solution to Luke's wealth ethics.[21] I shall describe and discuss that solution in greater detail later. For the present, it is enough to offer two reasons, directly connected with 14:33, why I do not consider it plausible and accordingly why I believe that Luke should in fact be seen in this verse (as elsewhere) to understand discipleship and divestiture of possessions as a soteriological requirement for all. First, as other scholars have noted,[22] Luke does not appear to have used the term "disciple" as a technical designation for any particular sub-group or class of believers. On the contrary, particularly in Acts, he uses it quite consistently as a synonym for "believers" (Acts 6:1, 2, 7; 9:1, 10, 19, 25–26, 29; 13:52; 14:20, 22, 28; 15:10; 16:1; 18:23, 27; 19:1, 9, 30, 20:1, 30: 21:4, 16). Second, as for example Tannehill has observed, Jesus' concluding remark in 14:33–35—"Let anyone with ears to hear listen!"—recalls the final comment in his telling of the parable of the sower in 8:4–8: ὁ ἔχων ὦτα ἀκούειν ἀκουέτω (8:8b; cf. 8:9–15).[23] This connects the two passages and invites the reader to interpret 14:33–35 in the light of 8:4–8 (and 8:9–15). And interestingly, in the latter of these texts, although he distinguishes between no fewer than four different types of responses to the word, Jesus identifies only one of these as appropriate, namely the one that yields "a hundred fold" (8:8a; cf. 8:15). The connection between these texts suggests that in 14:33–35, too, he must have perceived only one response to the gospel as acceptable. And that, of course, can only be discipleship (since that is the only type he mentions there).

If I am correct, then, 14:33 (cf. also 12:33) identifies a relinquishment of "all" as a soteriological requirement for everyone. But exactly what did Luke understand by "all" (πάντα) (cf. also 18:22)? Did he imply that believers would need to divest themselves of literally everything they owned in order to be saved? I believe that three factors, taken together, suggest that he should be construed in a slightly less radical fashion. First, like the other synoptics (Mk 1:37, 51; 23:5; Mt. 3:5; 4:24 23:5; 21:26), Luke frequently availed himself of hyperbole when using the

21 Hays, *Luke's Wealth Ethics*, esp. 3–6.
22 E.g., Seccombe, *Possessions and the Poor*, 104–5; Hays, *Luke's Wealth Ethics*, 4.
23 Tannehill, *Narrative Unity: Luke*, 149.

word πάντα (Lk. 5:17; 20:45; 21:17, 38; 22:70; Acts 1:1, 19; 9:35; 18:17; 19:10, 17; 21:28; 26:4). Thus, we have no a priori reason to suppose that he used the term in connection with divestiture in a way that should be taken entirely at face value.[24] Second, Luke's description of the disciples clearly indicates that we should not. In 5:11 and 5:28 he explains that Peter and Levi had abandoned "everything" for the sake of following Jesus. And in 18:28 Peter declares that each of the twelve had left τὰ ἴδια in a way that conforms to the commandment given to the rich ruler to abandon "all" (18:22); and evidently Jesus agrees. Yet Luke's portrayal of the twelve reveals that they had not in fact embraced an existence utterly without possessions, such as a literal reading would seem to imply. Passages such as 9:1–6, 9:10–17, and 22:35–38 demonstrate that even after their calling they normally carried modest amounts of money around with them as well as food and extra clothing, and some of them even swords.[25] Third, at various moments (cf., above all, 6:27–36; 11:41) Jesus exhorts his listeners to give alms. If, as most interpreters believe, Luke understood almsgiving as something to be performed repeatedly, and did not take it as a synonym for divestiture, then these exhortations would seem to be at odds with the commandments to relinquish "all," if indeed "all" should be understood literally. For clearly abandoning all in the straightforward sense of the term would leave one with nothing with which to continue to offer charity. As noted in the introduction to this chapter, several interpreters do in fact perceive a contradiction between these directives.[26] But if we allow for a measure of hyperbole in Luke's use of the word πάντα, the contradiction disappears. Then it becomes possible to understand Luke as demanding of believers an initial act of divestiture of "all," in a somewhat diluted sense of the term, and then in addition a commitment to subsequent acts of almsgiving.

On the other hand, we should hardly allow for too much hyperbole. The fact that everyone, not just the rich, is instructed to leave "all," suggests that the type of economic lifestyle that Luke considered appropriate for believers was significantly below average. Furthermore, his instruction in 12:22–31 to avoid concerns about the necessities of life

24 Cf. also Hays, *Luke's Wealth Ethics*, 82–84.
25 Cf., again, ibid., 81–100.
26 Cf. above all Mineshige, *Besitzverzicht und Almosengeben*.

would be difficult to reconcile with an acceptance of a possession of substantial amounts of money or belongings. Hence my contention above that, according to most texts in Luke's gospel, salvation requires an assumption of a "very modest" standard of living. I shall refrain from putting actual numbers to what "very modest" should be taken to imply, however. Luke' writing does not give us data for that kind of specificity.

The texts that we have so far reviewed give emphasis to different things, but are mutually coherent and may be seen to contribute to the verbalization of a unified ethical stance: the possession of wealth is unacceptable, and believers, if they are to be saved, must renounce their belongings for the benefit of the poor and adopt a very modest standard of living (or, alternatively, content themselves with such a standard if that is what they have). And furthermore, after they have done so, they must continue to give alms to those in need. The same is true of a number of other passages, for instance 16:14, where Luke accuses the Pharisees of "love for money," or φιλαργυρία, the numerous passages in which Jesus directly or indirectly identifies the impoverished as the prime recipients of the gospel (e.g., 4:18; 6:20–23; 7:22; 14:21; cf. 1:52–53), 21:1–4, where he praises the generosity of the poor widow, and 16:1–13, which gives us the parable of the dishonest steward (16:1–13). This last text is admittedly fraught with conundrums and may defy a fully satisfactory reading.[27] It is unclear, for instance (to me at least), whether the steward was guilty of the crime of which he stood accused;[28] whether in that case he had squandered only his own money or that of his master;[29] and whether in 16:5–7 he reduces principal or interest owed to his master or cancels commission due to himself.[30] Furthermore, it may be difficult to decide exactly how Jesus'

27 For a helpful history of research prior to the early 1990s see Ireland, *Stewardship and the Kingdom*, 5 47.

28 For the view that most likely he was not, see J. S. Kloppenborg, "The Dishonoured Master (Lk. 16:1–8a)," Bib. 70, no. 4 (1989): 488; Metzger (*Consumption and Wealth*, 111) and Wolter (*Lukasevangelium*, 545) posit that he probably was.

29 For the case that he had squandered his own money, see Metzger, *Consumption and Wealth*, 116; for the opposite reading, see H. Moxnes, *The Economy of the Kingdom: Social Conflict and Economic Relations in Luke's Gospel* (Philadelphia, PA: Fortress Press, 1988), 141; Johnson, *Luke*, 243; J. G. Lygre, "Of What Charges? (Lk. 16:1–2)," *BTB* 32, no. 1 (2002): 21–28.

30 Kloppenborg ("Dishonoured Master," 488–90) and R. S. Schellenberg ("Which Master? Whose Steward? Metalepsis and Lordship in the Parable of the Prudent

application of the parable in 16:8b–13 should be seen to cohere with the various details of the story? Despite these difficulties, however, it is clear that the passage as a whole ends on a note of sharp contrast between devotion to God and devotion to money, which may be seen to encourage both a relinquishment of possessions and a commitment to subsequent acts of charity. For after all, if "love for God" by necessity implies a "hatred of mammon," such as Jesus' final comment potently establishes, then arguably neither of these would seem too much to ask.

Since this perspective is conveyed by the majority of texts dealing with belongings, I shall refer to it in the rest of this chapter as the gospel's dominant outlook on possessions. But as noted, there are a minority of passages that deviate from it and suggest that the possession of wealth may in fact be compatible with the attainment of salvation. Chief among these are 14:12–14 and 19:1–10. Let us briefly review each of these, again starting with the last.

Luke 19:1–10 gives us the story of Jesus' encounter with Zacchaeus. On his way to Jerusalem Jesus passes through Jericho surrounded by a large crowd of people. Zacchaeus, a chief tax collector, is eager to see him, but unable to do so on account of his modest height (19:3).[31] He therefore dashes ahead of Jesus and the crowd and climbs a sycamore tree to get a better view. From afar Jesus greets him and invites himself over to visit his house. Zacchaeus reacts by descending from the tree, receiving him as his guest, and (in response to the misgivings of the townspeople; cf. 19:7) making the following promise, "Look, half of my possessions, Lord, I will give to the poor; and if I have defrauded anyone of anything,

Steward [Lk. 16.1–13]," *JSNT* 30, no. 3 [2008]: 263–88) suggest principal or interest, whereas Fitzmyer (Luke X–XXIV, 1097–8) and Metzger (*Consumption and Wealth*, 122) argue for commission.

31 The crowd may also have been disinclined to make way for him given his status as a sinner; cf. J. B. Green, "Good News to Whom? Jesus and the 'Poor' in the Gospel of Luke," in *Jesus of Nazareth: Lord and Christ. Essays on the Historical Jesus and New Testament Christology*, ed. J. B. Green and M. Turner (Grand Rapids, MI: Eerdmans, 1994), 71. M. C. Parsons ("'Short in Stature': Luke's Physical Description of Zacchaeus," *NTS* 47, no. 1 [2001]: 50–57) suggests that Luke's mention of Zacchaeus' shortness should be viewed against the background of ancient physiognomy, where "shortness of height" would be seen to correspond to "small-mindedness." Luke, in Parson's assessment, invokes this assumption in order to subvert it through the following narrative.

I will repay them four times as much" (ἰδοὺ τὰ ἡμίσιά μου τῶν ὑπαρχόντων, κύριε, τοῖς πτωχοῖς δίδωμι, καὶ εἴ τινός τι ἐσυκοφάντησα ἀποδίδωμι τετραπλοῦν) (19:8). To this, Jesus approvingly replies, "Today salvation (σωτηρία) has come to this house, because he, too, is a son of Abraham. For the Son of Man came to seek out and to save the lost" (19:9–10).

There can be no doubt, of course, that Zacchaeus' promise is generous. Few would have done what he pledges to do.[32] Even so, in the light of the passages so far reviewed—not least 18:18–30, which is only about half a chapter away—Jesus' immediate "counter-promise" of salvation may take the reader by surprise. Like the rich ruler, Zacchaeus is described as a man of wealth (19:2, πλούσιος; although admittedly the ruler is described as "very rich," πλούσιος σφόδρα). Yet unlike the rich ruler, he learns that he, and his house, will be able to obtain salvation at the price of a divestiture of only half of his possessions, plus extras. The contrast between τὰ ἡμίσια in 19:8 and πάντα in 18:22 is remarkable, and Jesus' answer to Zacchaeus is very difficult to fit into what I describe as the gospel's dominant outlook on possessions. It appears to allow for a considerably more comfortable standard of living than Luke's Jesus normally does.

It has admittedly been suggested that the difference between 18:18–30 (and the other texts analysed above) and 19:1–10 is negligible. Tannehill, for instance, has argued that in 19:1–10 Luke implies that Zacchaeus had deceived so many that after he had relinquished half of his possessions and compensated the victims of his fraud, he would be left "pretty much in the same financial state required of the rich ruler."[33] Thus, for him, too, salvation should be seen to have been available only at the cost of a full divestiture.[34] This is possible, of course, although in my assess-

32 For apt criticism of the view that in 19:8 Zacchaeus should be describing an on-going practice on his part rather than formulating a promise for the future, espoused in, e.g., A. C. Mitchell, "Zacchaeus Revisited: Lk. 19,8 as a Defense," *Bib.* 71 (1990): 153–76; D. A. S. Ravens, "Zacchaeus: The Final Part of a Lucan Triptych?" *JSNT* 41 (1991): 19–32; Green, *Luke*, 670–1, see D. Hamm, "Lk. 19:8 Once Again: Does Zacchaeus Defend or Resolve?" *JBL* 107, no. 3 (1988): 431–37; Mineshige, *Besitzverzicht und Almosengeben*, 200 n. 414; Hays, *Luke's Wealth Ethics*, 177.

33 Tannehill, *Narrative Unity: Luke*, 124.

34 Metzger (*Consumption and Wealth*, 175–6) has opted for continuity between 18:18–30 and 19:1–10 on the grounds that in 19:8 Luke places μου after τὰ ἡμίσια rather than after τῶν ὑπαρχόντων. This, he suggests, implies that Zacchaeus promised to donate

ment not very likely. Luke nowhere suggests as much, and the contrast between τὰ ἡμίσια and πάντα would then appear to needlessly complicate his rhetoric. Why not simply say that Zacchaeus had promised to give everything away while earmarking some of his funds for those that he had defrauded if that is in fact what he wanted to communicate? In any case, even if Tannehill's reading is viable, it remains that the passage leaves Luke's readers free to conclude that other rich people who had not defrauded anyone would be able to reach salvation by relinquishing only half of their property.

Luke 19:1–10 thus intimates that the possession of wealth need not work as an impediment to salvation. For many rich people, relinquishing half would still leave them reasonably wealthy (Seneca, for instance, to take an extreme case, would be left with around 150,000,000 sesterces, according to the data provided by Dio Chrysostom in 61.33.10). Luke 14:12–14 moves even further in that direction, and thus further away from the gospel's general outlook on possessions. In this passage Jesus has been invited to dine in the house "of one of the leaders of the Pharisees" (τινος τῶν ἀρχόντων τῶν Φαρισαίων) (14:1). And after having healed a man suffering from dropsy (14:2–6) and instructed his surroundings on the appropriateness of humility (14:7–11), he offers his host the following advice,

> When you give a dinner or a banquet, do not invite your friends or your brothers or your relatives or rich neighbours, in case they may invite you in return, and you would be repaid. But when you give a feast, invite the beggars, the crippled, the lame, and the blind. And you will be blessed (καὶ μακάριος ἔσῃ), because they cannot repay you, for you

not half of his possessions, but rather *his* half of the sum total of possessions owned by the members of his household together. On that reading, Zacchaeus might be seen, in conformity with 18:22, to have vowed to relinquish everything he owned. This reading fails to take two matters into account. First, in 9:9, as we have seen, Jesus promises salvation to the whole of Zacchaeus' household. This would seem odd if certain members of this household were in possession of significant funds, but unlike Zacchaeus had not (yet) pledged to relinquish them. Second, if Zacchaeus did promise to give all of his possessions to the poor, it follows that he would not have had much left with which to compensate the victims of his fraud (unless, of course, we are to assume a very liberal understanding of "all," which, incidentally, Metzger does not).

> will be repaid at the resurrection of the righteous (ἀνταποδοθήσεται γάρ σοι ἐν τῇ ἀναστάσει τῶν δικαίων).

From the narrative context and the content of 14:12–13, it is clear that the person to whom he is speaking is a man of considerable means. Even so, Jesus nowhere demands of this man that he divest himself of all or even half of his property for the benefit of the poor. On the contrary, he suggests that if only he will show himself willing to invite the poor and the maimed—those at the bottom of the social order—into his home when giving a dinner party, and bracket the *quid-pro-quo* logic of conventional forms of social intercourse,[35] he will be counted among the blessed on the day of retribution.[36]

The above survey has yielded the following picture. Generally speaking, Luke's gospel conveys the message that wealth is incompatible with salvation and that believers in order to be saved must renounce all of their belongings (in the slightly weakened sense of "all" previously defined) and adopt a very modest standard of living, and additionally continue to give alms to those in need. A minority of texts, however, deviate from this view and suggest that material wealth may be compatible with salvation. One of these, 19:1–10, indicates that a mere fifty per cent divestiture may be enough, even for the rich, to earn redemption; another, 14:12–14, that the rich may "get away" with as little as a display of hospitality to the socially disadvantaged. With this summary in the back of our minds, let us now proceed to Acts.[37]

35 Cf., e.g., Moxnes, *Economy of the Kingdom*, 129–34.

36 Luke's use of the word μακάριος in this text is interesting, and surprising, given that in 6:20–26, in the Sermon on the Plain, he had categorically opposed the rich to the group that he identified there as "blessed."

37 One might perhaps also point to 3:10–14 and 8:2–3 as deviating from the gospel's dominant outlook. In the former of these texts, John the Baptist offers instruction to a group of people on how to avoid divine judgment. Absent from his teaching are any condemnation of wealth and any mention of the need for a divestiture of possessions. Instead, his focus lies on sharing and other more "conventional" forms of just behaviour, "And the crowds asked him, 'What then should we do?' In reply he said to them, 'Whoever has two coats must share with anyone who has none; and whoever has food should do the same.' Even tax collectors came to be baptized, and they asked him, 'Teacher, what should we do?' He said to them, 'Collect no more than the amount prescribed for you.' Soldiers also asked him, 'And we, what should we do?' He said to them, 'Do not extort money from anyone by threats

As noted, we shall return to Luke's depiction of the first congregation in Jerusalem at the end of the chapter. In this section we therefore confine ourselves to discussing the chapters that follow on the disbandment of the *Urgemeinde* at the beginning of Acts 8. Coming from the gospel, Luke's approach to belongings in this part of his work is surprising. We noted above, in connection with our analysis of Luke 12:13–21, that Luke's Jesus warns his listeners against "all kinds of greed" (cf. also Luke's charge against the Pharisees of φιλαργυρία in 16:14). Denunciation of avarice continues in Acts 8–28, although frequently it is delivered here in a slightly less overt fashion than in the gospel (8:18–24; 16:16–24; 19:18–19; 24:25–26). Similarly, this portion of his work also encourages almsgiving, as does the gospel, as we have seen. In 20:34–35, for instance, in his speech to the elders of Ephesus, Paul stipulates charity to the "weak." And in several passages Luke speaks in romanticizing ways of people who engage in almsgiving (9:36–43; 10:2; 11:29; 24:17). Yet noticeably absent from this segment of his work are any critique of wealth and any mention of divestiture, whether a full or a partial one, of possessions. This absence is particularly noteworthy given that Acts 8–28 features a number of conversions of members of the comfortable and even of the highest levels of society. We may mention the Ethiopian eunuch (8:26–39), the Roman commander Cornelius (10:1–48), the Roman governor and senator Sergius Paulus (13:6–12), the seller of purple goods Lydia (16:11–15), the "not so few" leading (cf. πρώτων) women in Thessalonica (17:4), the equally "not so few" notables (cf. εὐσχημόνων) in Beroea (17:12), and the Areopagite Dionysius (17:34). Interestingly, none of these is reported to

or false accusation, and be satisfied with your wages'" (3:10–14). In the latter we hear of a group of female believers who allegedly "provided for" Jesus and the disciples "out of their own resources" (8:3). It is difficult to say exactly how much money these women should be thought to have possessed. But the fact that they were able to support Jesus and his followers for an extended period of time and that one of them, Joanna, is described as "the wife of Herod's steward Chuza" (8:3) yield the impression of their funds, or at least the funds of some of them, being quite substantial. Nevertheless, none of these is ever asked, let alone commanded, to divest themselves of their means. However, since these women may theoretically be regarded as gradually divesting themselves of their funds through the support that they provide, and since the instructions in 3:10–14 are spoken "only" by John, not Jesus (who must, after all, be regarded as the gospel's main carrier of Luke's teaching), one may perhaps be justified in downplaying the significance of these texts.

have renounced their property, or any portion of it, in connection with or after their adoption of the Christian faith. And nowhere does Luke suggest through any of his characters or his own narrative voice that this should be problematic.

This absence, of course, has not gone unnoticed in the scholarly literature.[38] Few, however, have taken it to imply that Luke's view of possessions had changed from the time that he wrote the gospel to the time that he wrote the Acts. Some have even argued against such an idea. Hays, for instance, has proposed that Luke says nothing about divestiture in Acts 8–28 simply because the sources that were available to him on the period covered by these chapters did not contain any stories about divestiture and that Luke "[a]s an historian … [was] not at liberty to fabricate [any] such"—although clearly this would have been "in keeping with his moralising agenda."[39] This may seem an odd proposal, however, given that nothing in Luke's writings suggests that he should have felt under any particular obligation to demonstrate loyalty to his sources and that Hays elsewhere rather keenly emphasizes Luke's freedom as a writer. Notice, for instance, his severe critique of K.-J. Kim on p. 180, where he stresses the need to appreciate "Luke's literary acuity."[40] Hays also suggests that Luke may not have intended his readers to perceive the converts of these chapters as actual *Identifikationsfiguren*, at least not in all respects. Lydia, for instance, may have been invoked as a role model with regard to hospitality, and Cornelius with regard to almsgiving, but neither of these should be seen as role models with respect to possessions generally.[41] It may be difficult to grasp, however, why Luke should have chosen to speak of these figures only with commendation, as indeed he does, if at the same time he wished for his audience to decode them as deficient and decidedly non-exemplary in certain rather vital moral respects.

For me, at least, it is therefore difficult to avoid the conclusion that the absence in Acts 8–28 of any condemnation of wealth and any mention of divestiture suggests that Luke's view of possessions had indeed

38 Cf., e.g., Mineshige, *Besitzverzicht und Almosengeben*, 252–3, and the discussion of previous research in the following section.

39 Hays, *Luke's Wealth Ethics*, 250.

40 Cf. Kim, *Stewardship and Almsgiving*, 109.

41 Hays, *Luke's Wealth Ethics*, 251.

developed from the time that he wrote the gospel to the time that he wrote Acts, and that in the latter work, unlike in most parts of the former, he aimed to signal that the possession of wealth is acceptable and compatible with life as a Christian and not a hindrance to the attainment of salvation.

My own understanding of the reason behind this development in Luke's thought, and of the discrepancies in the gospel itself, will be the subject of a later section in this chapter. Before we get to that, however, let us review the ways in which previous scholarship has attempted to make sense of the incongruities outlined here.

Previous Research

In the previous section I delineated my own perception of the passages in Luke's volumes that deal with possessions, exempting those concerned with the first congregation in Jerusalem. The discussions showed, among other things, that there is no scholarly consensus about the understanding of these. However, most interpreters at least agree that Luke seems to have given expression to different views and demands in different passages in his work. In some he stipulates a divestiture of all, in some a divestiture of only fifty per cent, in some he requires almsgiving, and in some he demands nothing more than hospitality to those at the bottom of the social order.[42] Similarly, in some passages he categorically condemns the possession of wealth, whereas in others he seems to condone it. Most interpreters also agree that on the surface at least this appears contradictory. Many have argued, however, that it is possible to discover a coherent ethical stance beneath the contradictions. In this section I shall examine the ways in which scholars have variously tried to do so. In partial reliance on Hays, I divide the attempts that have been made (including his own) into four categories (bi-vocational, interim, personalist, and symbolic solutions) and discuss each of these in turn.[43] My aim will be to show that none of these is compelling, and that we should

42 As noted, however, I personally do not perceive a contradiction between the demands concerning almsgiving and a divestiture of everything.

43 Cf. Hays, *Luke's Wealth Ethics*, esp. 1–24.

therefore probably content ourselves with the notion that the contradictions are real.

Bi-vocational. In 1965 H.-J. Degenhardt published the first specialized study on Luke's ethics of possessions. In this work he recognized the heterogeneity of Luke's teaching, but argued that the diversity should be seen to reflect not a lack of consistency in Luke's thinking on the subject, but a conviction that different requirements apply to different persons. In Degenhardt's view, Luke thus distinguished between two different groups of believers, "the disciples" (οἱ μαθηταί) and "the people" (ὁ λαός). The former were the inner circle around Jesus, and prefigured the later full-time ministers of the church (*die Amtsträger*). The latter were Christ believers in general. According to Degenhardt, the most radical demands of Luke's writings (i.e., those involving a divestiture of all) should be seen as directed exclusively at "disciples," and *Amtsträger*, and the other rather more lenient ones at "the people."[44]

I have already offered two reasons why I do not consider this reading viable. First, the lexicographical distinction between μαθηταί and λαός is untenable. Luke often employs the term "disciples" of ordinary believers. Second, the intratextual connection between Luke 14:33–35 and 8:4–15 suggests that the author understood discipleship as the only appropriate form of Christian existence. But let me at this moment adduce a few more reasons. Third, Degenhardt's perception requires that Luke nowhere condemns the rich generally, but only those rich who either reject the gospel or attempt to assume discipleship without being willing to pay the price of divestiture.[45] But as we have seen, Luke frequently condemns the rich without any such qualifications (cf. Lk. 1:52–53; 6:24–26; 12:13–21; 18:25; 16:19–31). And fourth, the story of the rich ruler seems to decisively work against it (18:18–34). This man was instructed to renounce all of his possessions despite the fact that all that he had asked for was salvation, not discipleship. Naturally, one could argue that this was so because Jesus also summoned him to discipleship (cf. 18:22, καὶ δεῦρο ἀκολούθει μοι).[46] But that only begs the question why discipleship should be necessary for the salvation of this particular individual when appar-

44 Degenhardt, *Evangelist der Armen*, esp. 27–41.

45 Cf. ibid., 53.

46 Cf. ibid., 143; Hays, *Luke's Wealth Ethics*, 179.

ently it was not for others. As noted, we have little reason to think that Luke understood this man as "a special case."

K.-J. Kim has offered a solution largely similar to the one advocated by Degenhardt. The main difference is that he discriminates not between οἱ μαθηταί and ὁ λαός, but between "itinerant" and "sedentary" disciples, as he terms them.[47] This modification successfully bypasses the first problem connected with Degenhardt's reading, but hardly the other three.[48]

Interim. Whereas advocates of the bi-vocational view attempt to dissolve Luke's inconsistencies by distinguishing between different categories of believers, supporters of the interim solution do so by distinguishing between different historical eras. This solution comes in a variety of forms. Most of these agree, however, that Luke understood his most radical demands to have been pertinent only in the past. G. Theißen, W. Horn, and W. Stegemann, for instance, thus all speak of Luke 22:35–38 as a watershed moment of the history of the church.[49] Prior to this point, divestiture of πάντα was required of all believers. But in these verses, shortly before his departure from this world, Jesus inaugurates a new era in the history of Christianity subject to a more lenient ethical regime. Mineshige accepts this view, but adds a further distinction between the era of the early church (Acts 1–7), when sharing of possessions was compulsory, and the era of Luke's own day (Acts 8–28 and beyond), when only charity and hospitality were required.[50] Petracca alternatively suggests that Luke understood divestiture of all as obligatory not specifically during the time of Jesus, but rather for his eyewitnesses (whose lives and activities were, of course, limited to a certain historical period, though).[51] A last scholar to be mentioned here is D. P. Seccombe. He

47 Kim, *Stewardship and Almsgiving*, 102–9.

48 Kim's distinction between itinerant and sedentary disciples strongly resembles the one developed by Theißen between "die Wandercharismatiker" and "die Sympathisanten in den Ortsgemeinden"; cf. above all G. Theißen, *Soziologie der Jesusbewegung: Eine Beitrag zur Entstehungsgeschichte des Urchristentums*, Theologische Existenz Heute 194 (Munich: Kaiser, 1977), 14–32. Kim, though, acknowledges no debt to Theißen at this point.

49 G. Theißen, "Wanderradikalismus: Literatursoziologische Aspekte der Überlieferung von Worten Jesu im Urchristentum," *ZTK* 70 (1973): esp. 270; Horn, *Glaube und Handeln*, 197–8; Schottroff and Stegemann, *Hoffnung der Armen*, 89–153.

50 Mineshige, *Besitzverzicht und Almosengeben*, 263–4.

51 Petracca, *Gott oder das Geld*, 326; cf. Countryman, *Rich Christian in the Church*, 132.

suggests that Luke discriminated between "extreme" and "ordinary" situations and regarded divestiture of all as compulsory only in the former. He notices that Jesus articulates the majority of his radical imperatives and views in connection with the Travel Narrative (9:51–19:28) and contends that at that time he expected his followers to die with him in Jerusalem.[52] According to Seccombe, Luke considered divestiture of everything as mandatory for believers in extreme situations such as this, as an appropriate expression of true discipleship. But in normal situations, such as that of his own day, this type of conduct would be unnecessary. In Luke's assessment, however, so Seccombe argues, extreme situations could arise again, for instance if persecutions of believers should suddenly break out. And this would inaugurate a new era of radical demands.

For all their differences, these proposals all come up against the same problem: their incapacity to explain why certain individuals both living in the time of Jesus and being eyewitnesses to him (and meeting him at a point during the Travel Narrative) were promised or offered salvation without being required to relinquish all (cf. 14:12–14; 19:1–10). Furthermore, we should add that Luke 22:35–38 does not, as is frequently believed, lend itself easily to an interim reading. Scholars who argue so commonly contend that Jesus here inaugurates a new era of more moderate ethical demands by authorizing his disciples, as of that moment, to own more than they had previously done. But that is a misreading. All that Jesus does in that passage is to direct those of his disciples already in possession of purses and bags to bring these along with them (unlike what they had done in connection with their being sent away in Luke 9, which was clearly defined there as an exceptional situation), and those not in possession of swords to sell their cloaks and buy some. Thus, no net increase in the sum of their belongings can be seen. Furthermore, Jesus does not seem to be concerned in this text with the general future, as the interim reading requires, but only with the very immediate one. The citation of Isaiah 53:12 in Luke 22:37 and the remainder of the narrative clearly demonstrates that what Jesus aims to achieve in these verses

52 Seccombe, *Possessions and the Poor*, 97–222, esp. 116.

is to prepare, or indeed equip, his disciples for his own pending arrest, not to offer instructions about the time after his departure.[53]

Personalist. The bi-vocational and interim solutions are systematic in the sense that they suggest that different sets of imperatives can be matched with certain easily definable groups of believers or eras in the history of the church. The personalist approach is less "orderly." It suggests that Luke presented an array of requirements each of which he considered appropriate for different sorts of people. This proposition has been advanced by H.-J. Klauck, who suggests that Luke should have seen "umfassender Besitzverzicht" as only "eine Option unter anderen,"[54] and H.-G. Gradl, who speaks of a multiplicity of "legitime *Spielräume* und *Verwirklichungsmöglichkeiten*."[55] Neither of these scholars suggests that Luke should have left his readers at liberty to choose whatever instructions in his writings they might personally feel attracted to. But they do hold that the question of who should submit to which policies is impossible to settle through facile reference to the categorizations invoked by the supporters of the bi-vocational or interim views. Gradl proposes that it must be resolved in each case through guidance of the Spirit.[56] And Klauck contends that "Wer zu welcher Zeit und auf welche Weise handeln soll, das dürfte ... für Lukas weitgehend abhängig sein von den persönlichen Lebensumständen des Betreffenden und von der jeweiligen Situation, in die er sich gestellt sieht."[57] Hays' reading comes strikingly close to those of Klauck and Gradl, although on the surface it seems to differ. Hays proposes that Luke understood the commandment of 14:33 as relevant for all believers. But at the same time he argues that Luke perceived this commandment to subsume within itself every single injunction about property given by Jesus and the apostles and every type of behaviour assumed in that regard by any who accepts the gospel in the course of his works. In his assessment, the commandment thus expresses

53 Cf. also T. E. Schmidt, *Hostility to Wealth in the Synoptic Gospels*, JSNTsup 15 (Sheffield: JSOT Press, 1987), 160–1; Hays, *Luke's Wealth Ethics*, 93–100.
54 H.-J. Klauck, "Die Armut der Jünger in der Sicht des Lukas," in *Gemeinde, Amt, Sakrament: Neutestamentliche Perspektiven* (Würzburg: Echter, 1989), 193.
55 Gradl, *Arm und Reich*, 410; also quoted in Hays, *Luke's Wealth Ethics*, 19.
56 Gradl, *Arm Und Reich*, 130–1.
57 Klauck, "Armut der Jünger," 192.

"a coherent ethical principle with a range of contingent applications."[58] For some "renouncing all" implies relinquishing literally everything. For others it implies surrendering only fifty per cent. For others still it implies nothing more than almsgiving or the extension of hospitality. Like Klauck and Gradl, Hays submits that Luke does not leave his readers free to select just any type of behaviour that they might find appealing.[59] On the contrary, he claims that the precise form of approach that each believer must take toward property should be seen to depend on the nature of his or her calling and level of affluence.

Like the other approaches so far assessed, the personalist view comes across as unsatisfactory. Three reasons may be adduced. First, like the bi-vocational solution it fails to make sense of the fact that Luke repeatedly condemns not only *some* rich individuals, but rather *the* rich generically, without pointing to any exceptions. Second, on the assumption of the personalist model, it is difficult to see how Luke could have expected his audience to use his texts for moral guidance, since, as Klauck, Gradl, and Hays all concede, he nowhere clarifies exactly who should be seen to be subject to what requirements, or explicitly states what principles should be used in settling that question. Third, although it is clear that Luke gives expression to different demands in different portions of his work, he nowhere specifies that any of these should be seen as relevant only for some. To suggest that he intended this, without being capable of demonstrating that he indicated as much, is, as far as I can see, to presume what the solution claims to establish, namely that Luke did not contradict himself.

58 Hays, *Luke's Wealth Ethics*, 185 (de-italicized); cf. also 101, 267.

59 In this, they all differ from J. L. Gonzáles (*Faith and Wealth: A History of Early Christian Ideas on the Origin, Significance, and Use of Money* [San Francisco, CA: Harper & Row, 1990], who also offers a personalist approach. On p. 79 he writes that according to Luke, "[p]erfect discipleship entails renunciation of goods one could otherwise possess. For others who are not ready to go that far, [he] offers a number of examples of prosperous people whose encounter with Jesus led them to repentance and to sharing their possessions: the wealthy women who supported Jesus and his followers (Lk. 8:2–3) and the chief tax collector, who upon meeting Jesus decided to give half of his wealth to the poor and to return to any whom he had defrauded four times as much as he took from them." Gonzáles, though, nowhere clarifies where he finds evidence for a notion of voluntariness in Luke's teaching, or for a distinction between "perfect" and "imperfect" (?) discipleship.

Symbolic. A final strategy to be discussed in this section suggests that Luke's speech on possessions should not be construed in purely economic terms, as most interpreters do. This approach was pioneered in 1977 by L. T. Johnson in his monograph *The Literary Function of Possessions in Luke-Acts*. In this work he proposed that the attitudes to wealth of Luke's characters must be decoded as figurative expressions of their attitudes toward Jesus. Johnson discovers what he identifies as a "people and the prophet pattern" in Luke, which establishes a line of continuity between Jesus and the most prominent prophets of the Old Testament literature. Within this pattern "[t]he expressions rich and poor function … as metaphorical expressions for those rejected and accepted because of their response to the prophet."[60] Johnson suggests that Luke's metaphorical use of money talk extends into the early chapters of Acts, where the first Christians' subjection of their property to the apostles signifies their acknowledgement of the apostles' superior status.[61] Johnson, however, concedes that symbolic interpretation does not exhaust the meaning of Luke's utterances on belongings.[62] He maintains that Luke was painfully aware of the "literal power" that possessions exert "in centering and dominating men's lives."[63] He never clarifies, however, how the figurative and literal levels in Luke's speech on possessions should be seen to relate to one another.

Another interpreter to see symbolism at work in Luke's discourse on possessions is Seccombe. Unlike Johnson, however, he perceives symbolism only in Luke's use of the terms πρωχός and πλούσιος and only in the early chapters of the gospel. Seccombe notices that in the books of Isaiah and the Psalms—writings which, he remarks, "had a disproportionate influence on Luke"[64]—the authors use the noun πτωχός to refer to Israel as suppressed by its enemies and in need of salvation, and suggests that in the early parts of Luke the word should be seen to carry essentially the same meaning. Hence in 1:46–55, 4:16–30, and 6:17–49 the noun πτωχοί denotes not the financially deprived, as one might have expected,

60 Johnson, *Literary Function of Possessions*, 140.
61 Ibid., 213.
62 Ibid., 221.
63 Ibid., 159.
64 Seccombe, *Possessions and the Poor*, 94.

but those members of the chosen people who long for deliverance from the present aeon and accordingly respond favourably to Jesus' message. Conversely, the πλούσιοι are those who, "satisfied with the good things of this age," reject it.[65] As noted, Seccombe does not understand all of Luke's utterances on belongings as figurative. For instance, he interprets all occurrences of πτωχός and πλούσιος subsequent to Luke 6:49 and all of Jesus' various commandments on possessions literally. He never explains how these figurative and literal parts of Luke's discourse are meant to fit together.

Another symbolic, or quasi-symbolic, approach has been taken by J. B. Green. In an article from 1994 he performs what may be defined as a metonymic interpretation of Luke's use of πτωχός and πλούσιος. Green does not (always; cf. below on Zacchaeus) divest these terms of their ordinary literal meaning, but supplies them with a wider range of significance. Thus, he claims that in Luke the word πτωχός designates not only the impoverished, but rather anyone of "dishonorable status," i.e., anyone outside the Jewish "circles of power and prestige."[66] Clearly, according to Green, the πτωχοί include the impoverished, but also, for instance, the widows, the gentiles, and those who are otherwise unclean. Conversely, the πλούσιοι are the members of the Jewish elite. Green accordingly proposes that although on the surface Luke identifies Zacchaeus as a "rich" individual, he should be seen as a πτωχός, given that as a tax collector he was considered dishonourable by the members of the Jewish in-group.[67]

Scholars who espouse symbolic approaches to Luke's treatment of possessions rarely do so specifically with a view to dissolving the inconsistencies in his teaching. An exception may be R. F. O'Toole,[68] who manages to establish some sort of coherence in Luke's works by classifying all of the gospel's condemnations of the rich and all of its various injunctions about divestiture as metaphorical, while at the same time retaining a literal understanding of all the other passages concerning

65 Ibid., 95.
66 Green, "Good News to Whom?" 68; cf. also Lehtipuu, "The Rich, the Poor, and the Promise."
67 Green, "Good News to Whom?" 72.
68 R. F. O'Toole, *The Unity of Luke's Theology: An Analysis of Luke-Acts*, GNS 9 (Wilmington, DE: M. Glazier, 1984), 129–35.

possessions. He never elucidates how such a "bifurcated hermeneutic" might be justified, however. I point to the symbolic strategy here because it occupies a central place in the history of the interpretation of Luke's utterances on possessions and because it might be worth considering whether it could potentially help us discover a line of continuity in his thinking. The results, however, are disappointing. None of the readings referenced above seems viable. Neither Johnson nor Seccombe or O'Toole are able (or even attempts) to clarify how what they understand as the figurative and non-figurative parts or aspects of Luke's discourse on possessions may be seen to cohere with each other. This significantly weakens the credibility of their analyses. And clearly the interpretation of Green founders on exegetical unlikelihood. It is very difficult to grasp why Luke should have chosen to identify a man whom he wished for his audience to perceive as a πτωχός as in fact a πλούσιος.

The survey conducted in this section has shown that none of the attempts that have been made to dissolve the inconsistencies in Luke's teaching on wealth has been successful. It is possible, of course, that new and more satisfying approaches will be developed in the future. At the present moment, however, I deem it sensible to conclude that the inconsistencies delineated in the first part of the chapter are genuine. I therefore propose that we cease expending our energies on trying to dissolve these inconsistencies and dedicate them instead to trying to explain why they are there. In the following section, I attempt to do just that.

Toward an Explanation

Let me for the sake of clarity open this section by very briefly summarizing our findings in the first one. According to most texts in the gospel dealing with belongings, the possession of material wealth is incompatible with salvation, which requires a divestiture of "all" (in a slightly hyperbolical sense) for the benefit of the poor, and the adoption of a very modest standard of living, as well as continued offerings of charity to those in need. I have referred to this as the gospel's dominant outlook on possessions. According to a minority of passages, however, wealth and salvation need not be mutually exclusive. One of these suggests that the rich may retain half of their property and still be eligible for salvation;

another that they may hold on to all of it as long as they show hospitality to the poor and the maimed. In Acts 8–28 Luke continues to encourage almsgiving, but any talk of divestiture has evaporated. In these chapters he conveys that wealth and salvation may well be combined.

To a very large extent, I have already offered my own explanation for these various inconsistencies. My understanding of Luke's original purpose (or one of his purposes) in beginning to write a story of the life of Jesus and the history of the early church (namely his ambition to induce Theophilus to follow up on his conversion to the Christian belief by renouncing his position in society and adopting an essentially ascetic form of living) combined with my theory of Theophilus' reaction to his gospel after it had been released is able to account for the development we witness from the gospel's general outlook on possessions to the stance on the topic conveyed in Acts 8–28. But it is clear that the model stands in need of a little refinement, for in its present form it fails to make sense of the few texts in the gospel that deviate from its general outlook on possessions, above all 14:12–14 and 19:1–10. How might we account for these?

My answer is relatively "low tech." I suggest that, although through his gospel Luke had aimed to encourage Theophilus to renounce his affluence and embrace "a very modest standard of living," he realized from the outset both that Theophilus might not be easily convinced, and that he himself was not prepared to risk losing him as a member of his congregation. Hence he chose to include in his gospel a few texts that communicate that less than a divestiture of "all" might in the end be sufficient for the attainment of salvation, the general thrust of the gospel notwithstanding. These passages, I propose, were intended by Luke to provide Theophilus with paradigms for less self-sacrificing forms of conduct with respect to possessions than the one prescribed by the gospel's dominant perspective, in the event that he could not be swayed by this latter one. If my analysis above of Acts 8–28 is correct, this section proves that he could not, and was not in fact even prepared to, accept a partial relinquishment of his property, such as 19:1–10 encourages. Hence the complete absence in this segment of his work of the theme of divestiture.

So far so good. But what about Acts 1–7? So far I have bracketed out Luke's portrayal in these chapters of the first congregation in Jerusalem.

It is time now—in the following section, which is also the last of this chapter—to remove the brackets and examine how this portrayal may be seen to fit in with the model sketched above about Luke's interactions with Theophilus

The First Congregation

Before we can do so directly, we need to examine two preliminary questions. Did Luke, as I have suggested in the introduction to this chapter, actually ascribe to the first believers a community of goods? And if he did, then did he portray participation in that community as mandatory?

The view that Luke portrayed the first Christians as practising a community of goods, i.e., a form of communal living in which its members renounced private ownership of everything they possessed for the benefit of the common good, is a very standard one in Lucan scholarship.[69] In recent years, however, some interpreters have rejected it and suggested that Luke portrayed them as instead realizing the philosophical ideal of true friendship.[70] According to this, friends in the true sense of the term are characterized by sharing everything they own and thus by "holding all things in common," just as Luke contends was the custom of the members of the early church (Acts 2:44; 4:32; cf. the popular saying κοινὰ τῶν φίλων, allegedly coined by Pythagoras; DL 8.10). However, the type of sharing involved in this was (typically) one of use, not ownership.[71] Friends, according to this line of thinking, retain private owner-

69 E. Troeltsch, *Die Soziallehren der christlichen Kirchen und Gruppen* (Tübingen: J.C.B. Mohr, 1923); Esler, *Community and Gospel*, 169; Johnson, *Acts*, 61–3; Tannehill, *Narrative Unity: Acts*, 43–47; B. J. Capper, "Reciprocity and the Ethics of Acts," in *Witness to the Gospel: The Theology of Acts*, ed. I. H. Marshall and D. Peterson (Grand Rapids, MI: Eerdmans, 1998), 499–518; J. Jervell, *Die Apostelgeschichte*, KEK 3 (Göttingen: Vandenhoeck & Ruprecht, 1998), 156; Marguerat, *First Christian Historian*, 121–3; Fitzmyer, *Acts*, 269, 313; Pervo, *Acts*, 94, etc.

70 S. Walton, "Primitive Communism in Acts? Does Acts Present the Community of Goods (2:44–45; 4:32–35) as Mistaken?" *EvQ* 80, no. 2 (2008): 99–111; Hays, *Luke's Wealth Ethics*, 190–211.

71 For rather more detailed analyses of the relevant sources see, e.g., A. C. Mitchell "The Social Function of Friendship in Acts 2:44–47 and 4:32–37," *JBL* 111, no. 2 (1992): 258–64; D. A. Hume "'Sharing All Things in Common': Narrative, Alienation,

ship of what they have, but allow each other unrestricted access to it (e.g., Arist. *Pol.* 1263a34–39; Cic. *Off.* 1.51; Sen. *Ben.* 7.4.1). Similarly, according to Walton and Hays, the members of the first congregation should be seen to have generally remained in possession of their belongings, but at the same time have systematically put everything at everyone's disposal. Walton and Hays recognize, of course, that Luke does speak of a selling off of private property and of a distribution of the proceeds within the community (2:45; 4:34–35), but argue that the fact that he does so while consistently using verbs in the imperfect suggests that he understood those members who had engaged in this practice (the affluent ones) to have done so repeatedly, and so in each case to have also held something back (at least until the very last one), since otherwise they would not have had anything left to sell on a later occasion. They also acknowledge that in 4:32 Luke claims that none of the members of the community "called any of his belongings his own" (τι τῶν ὑπαρχόντων αὐτῷ ἔλεγεν ἴδιον), but propose that this should be understood not in the sense that none of them claimed private ownership of his or her property, but in the sense that none of them focused on questions of ownership.

Walton and Hays' proposal is intriguing, but ultimately uncompelling. Two reasons may be adduced. First, in 2:45 and 4:35 Luke clearly suggests that all the members of the community (cf. πᾶσιν; ἑκάστῳ) received portions of the funds made available through the selling of the property of the rich. There is no reason to assume that πᾶσιν and ἑκάστῳ should not be thought to include those people who had formerly owned this property and so that their selling of it had in fact, for each individual, been a once-and-for-all event, which had left them just as dependent on donations from the community's common purse as everyone else. (Luke's use of the imperfect, as opposed to the aorist form, need imply nothing more than that he conceptualized the practice of liquidating property as customary in the early church, and hence as performed and experienced repeatedly by its members seen as a collective entity.) Second, it is noteworthy that when in 4:34 Luke claims that not a single "needy person" (ἐνδεής) could be found among the believers, he ascribes this state

and the Friendship Ethos in Acts 2:41–47 and 4:32–35," in *Law and Narrative in the Bible and in Neighbouring Ancient Cultures*, ed. K.-P. Adam, F. Avemarie, and D. Felsch, FAT 2.54 (Tübingen: Mohr Siebeck, 2012), 329–32.

of affairs explicitly to the practice of selling off property for the benefit of the common good. By contrast, he nowhere claims or even intimates that anyone was helped by access to the private possessions of others, as certainly one might have expected if Walton and Hays were correct. In sum, we therefore have no good reason to reject the traditional view. When in 2:44 and 4:32 Luke claimed that the members of the first congregation "held all things in common," we may safely assume that he intended by this to imply that they had renounced private ownership of all that they possessed for the sake of the common good.

Most commentators answer the second preliminary question identified above in the negative. Luke may indeed have indicated a certain measure of peer pressure within the community, but in the end, according to the narrative he provides, any participation in the congregation's community of sharing was strictly voluntary.[72] Most interpreters who take this stance point to Acts 5:1–11 as evidence. These verses give us the story of Ananias and Sapphira, who sold some property, but delivered only part of the proceeds to the apostles, and were afterwards struck dead at the feet of Peter on hearing his words of condemnation. But according to these interpreters, Peter's comment to Ananias in 5:4 demonstrates that the couple were punished not because they had failed to surrender everything, but because they had pretended to do so while in reality keeping something back, and so they lied to both God and the Holy Spirit (cf. also 5:3). The verse reads,

> While it [the property] remained unsold, did it not remain your own? And after it was sold, were not the proceeds at your disposal? How is it that you have contrived this deed in your heart (οὐχὶ μένον σοὶ ἔμενεν καὶ πραθὲν ἐν τῇ σῇ ἐξουσίᾳ ὑπῆρχεν; τί ὅτι ἔθου ἐν τῇ καρδίᾳ σου τὸ πρᾶγμα τοῦτο)?

72 I. H. Marshall, *The Acts of the Apostles: An Introduction and Commentary*, TNTC (Leicester; Grand Rapids, MI: Inter-Varsity; Eerdmans, 1980), 112; Horn, *Glaube und Handeln*, 47; Esler, *Community and Gospel*, 195–6; Johnson, *Acts*, 88; Witherington, *Acts*, 207–8, 213–20; Marguerat, *First Christian Historian*, 155–78; Mineshige, *Besitzverzicht und Almosengeben*, 232–4; Fitzmyer, *Acts*, 323; Pervo, *Acts*, 129, and a host of others.

Johnson's commentary is standard: "The sharing of goods, we see, was voluntary. Ananias neither had to sell nor to share. Not ownership of property is the fault, but conspiracy which shatters the unity of the church."[73] If only the couple had been straightforward about it, they would have been welcome to retain however much from the sale that they might have desired, or even refrain from selling the property in the first place. Both the property and the profits had been "theirs"—and so any surrender of either voluntary.

In my assessment, however, 5:1–11 proves precisely that participation in the community's "sharing of goods," including a renunciation of all private property, was mandatory, since three factors indicate that the couple were in fact punished not only because they had lied, but also because they had failed to relinquish everything they owned. First, as B. Capper and Hays have emphasized, the verb that Luke uses to designate their "leaving something aside," νοσφίζω, usually carries distinctly negative connotations. Suitable translations include "embezzle," "misappropriate," and "steal."[74] Whatever the nuance, the term is generally used to designate actions perceived as morally reprehensible. Second, the grammar of Peter's question to Ananias in 5:3 suggests that he understood not only the couple's dishonesty but also its "leaving something aside" as illicit and indeed diabolic. Thus, the τί ἐπλήρωσεν ὁ σατανᾶς τὴν καρδίαν σου governs both the ψεύσασθαί σε τὸ πνεῦμα τὸ ἅγιον and the νοσφίσασθαι ἀπὸ τῆς τιμῆς τοῦ χωρίου. This implies that in Peter's assessment Satan had been behind not only the couple's act of lying, but also their decision to retain part of the profits of the sale for themselves.[75] Third, throughout his "conversation" with Peter, Ananias never speaks. This means that what Peter perceived as deceitfulness on his part must have been his very act of leaving only some of the proceeds from the sale at his and the other apostles' feet. This is easily understandable if delivering everything was mandatory and Peter was aware that Ananias and Sapphira had embezzled some of the profits. But if surrendering all or even any of one's possessions was voluntary, Peter's reaction to Ananias

73 Johnson, *Acts*, 88.

74 B. Capper, "Holy Community of Life and Property amongst the Poor: A Response to Steve Walton," *EvQ* 80, no. 2 (2008): 122–4; Hays, *Luke's Wealth Ethics*, 214.

75 Ibid., 216.

must imply that leaving something at the feet of the apostles was a gesture appropriate only for those members of the community who surrendered all and that any who contributed less would need to do so in a different style, if he or she did not want to be accused of lying. This is possible, but hardly likely, since Luke never mentions the existence of two different ways of ceding property to the community and since it is hard to imagine why more than one should be thought to have been necessary. All of this suggests that participation in the community of goods was indeed compulsory in the first congregation, according to Luke's description. Therefore 5:4 should probably be given a different interpretation from the one usually offered. I propose, contrary to Johnson and others of similar views, that what Peter implied in that verse was not that Ananias would have been free to keep whatever he wanted from the sale of his property (if only he had not lied), but rather that since that property and the money that he had received for it had both been subject to his authority all the way through (cf. ἐν τῇ σῇ ἐξουσίᾳ), he himself would now need to take full responsibility for the way in which he had handled them, which, as we have seen, was not acceptable.

With these considerations behind us, let us now turn to the central issue of this section: how might Luke's portrayal of the first congregation be seen to fit in with the theory that I have sketched about Luke and Theophilus and the development of Luke's ethics from the gospel to the Acts? If the answers given above are correct, it might seem natural to infer that this portrayal is devastating to that theory. For if, as I have suggested, one of Luke's aims in writing his second volume was to authorize Theophilus to retain his wealth and continue the kind of life to which he had been accustomed, why should he have chosen to include in that volume an idealizing depiction of an early Christian congregation in which participation in a community of goods, including a full surrender of all private property, was mandatory, and in which any failure to comply with its principles was punished by instantaneous death? Would we not have to agree that the inclusion of such a depiction contributes to communicating the exact opposite message from the one that he should then be seen to be trying to get across? Not really, as I will attempt to show in the rest of this section. On my interpretation, Luke's portrayal of the first congregation was intended and designed to help him solve a problem that had emerged the moment he had decided to adapt his ethics in the second volume to the preferences of Theophilus.

It has been the subject of much debate as to what sources or historical models Luke may have drawn on for his description of the first congregation. It is clear, of course, and universally accepted that his assertion in 4:34 that not a single ἐνδεής could be found in the community echoes Deuteronomy 15:4 and thus represents life in the *Urgemeinde* as a realization of the commandment given in that verse. But most scholars believe that Luke was also bringing other material into play. As noted, some have pointed to the thoughts of the philosophers on the nature of true friendship. Others have spoken of (descriptions of) various Jewish communities such as that of Qumran, that of the Essenes, or that of the Therapeutae.[76] I do not wish to suggest that none of these may have played a formative role in Luke's description of the congregation. But I would like to point to a few differences between this and these possible sources of influence. We have already seen that Luke portrays the first Christians as sharing their possessions in a more fundamental manner than the one typically deemed suitable for φίλοι by the philosophers. And with regard to the Qumranites, the Essenes, and the Therapeutae, it is worth noticing that these were generally understood to have shared not only in the consumption of goods, but also in the production of goods, whereas Luke never speaks about any actual production.[77] On the contrary, he seems to imply that the members of the *Urgemeinde* were quite simply living off the donations of the rich.

For this and other reasons I am more persuaded by those who have pointed to descriptions of various mythical ages in the history of humanity in Greek and Roman literature (cf., e.g., Hes. *Op.* 109–201; Ov. *Met.*

76 Cf. Capper, "Reciprocity and the Ethics"; J. Taylor, "The Community of Goods among the First Christians and among the Essenes," in *Historical Perspectives: From the Hasmoneans to Bar Kokhba in Light of the Dead Sea Scrolls*, ed. D. M. Goodblatt, A. Pinnick, and D. R. Schwartz, STDJ 37 (Boston, MS.: Brill, 2001), 147–61. For an excellent clarification of why the Essenes should not be considered identical with the Qumranites see S. Mason *Josephus, Judea, and Christian Origins: Methods and Categories* (Peabody, MS: Hendrickson Publishers, 2009), 239–79.

77 Hence, as G. Hallbäck (*Apostlenes Gerninger Fortolket*, Det Danske Bibelselskabs Kommentarserie [Copenhagen: Det Danske Bibelselskab, 1993], 49) has noted, the term *Liebeskommunismus* coined by Troeltsch (*Soziallehren der christlichen Kirchen*, 49–50) is somewhat misleading.

1.88–150) as a prime source of inspiration.[78] In particular, I find references to Seneca's account of the so-called Second Age in his ninetieth letter to Lucilius apposite.

Luke's description of the first congregation resembles Seneca's description of the Second Age in a number of ways. Like the time of the first congregation, the Second Age, according to Seneca, was a period of idyll (cf. *fortunata tempora*) (*Ep.* 90.36); like the members of the first congregation, those living during the Second Age did not produce anything (90.36, 38, 40);[79] and like these members, they lived their lives together, in unity (cf. *consortio*) (90.36; cf. Acts 2:42, 44, 46; 4:32), while sharing everything (90.38, 40; cf. Acts 4:32, 34, 36–37), with the happy result that "you could not find a poor person among them," as Seneca puts it (*pauperem envire non posses*) (90.38; cf. Acts 4.34). Furthermore, there is a certain similarity between Seneca's description of the decline of the Second Age and Luke's description of the period immediately preceding the dissolution of the first community. As noted, Acts 5:1–11 gives us the story of Ananias and Sapphira, who greedily kept something back for their own private use. And shortly thereafter we hear of dissension within the community between the Hebrews and the Hellenists on account of the widows of the latter being neglected in the daily distribution. As argued in the introduction to this chapter, these widows came to experience hunger although the community appears to have had sufficient resources to satisfy the needs of all. It is noteworthy that, according to Seneca, the Second Age came to an end precisely when avarice (*avaritia*) arose among humans and people started to desire the possession of private property. Once this happened, the idyll was broken, and poverty soon ensued. Thus, in both Luke and Seneca we have a scenario where we see, first, the emergence of greed and then, afterwards, the arrival of need, and notably need in a situation where this ought not to have been necessary.

78 Above all D. Mealand, "Community of Goods and Utopian Allusions in Acts II–IV," *JTS* 28 (1977): 96–99; cf. also Capper, "Reciprocity and the Ethics"; Hays, *Luke's Wealth Ethics*, 205–8.

79 Seneca admittedly ascribes this not to anyone's selling of private property, but to the circumstance that the earth spontaneously brought forward food and other *beneficia naturae* (90.36, 38, 40).

Obviously, what we have between Luke and Seneca is not a perfect match. There are significant differences, as will be clear to anyone who reads the material. Most importantly, perhaps, Seneca claims that the Second Age came to an end solely as a result of inner disunity, whereas Luke asserts that the first congregation was finally dissolved through pressure from outside. In my assessment, however, the similarities listed above are remarkable enough to suggest that Luke could have consciously modelled his portrayal of the first congregation on Seneca's description of the Second Age, presumably while also reworking and reshuffling material he had inherited from the Christian tradition. And this, indeed, is what I propose he did.

But why, we may ask, should he have chosen to do so? To answer this question we need to briefly comment on the role of the Second Age in Seneca's moral philosophy. Naturally, we cannot engage in a detailed discussion of Seneca's ethics here. Fortunately, we do not need to. For present purposes, it is enough to note that although the Roman philosopher certainly speaks of the Second Age in a highly romanticizing fashion, he never ascribes to it any actual normative function for people of his own day.[80] Thus, we nowhere find Seneca suggesting that his own contemporaries should "hold all things in common" the way the people of the Second Age had done. For all his emphasis as a Stoic philosopher on the unity of humanity and on everyone's access to god's reason, or logos (and hence his emphasis on the appropriateness of *amicitia* between masters and slaves and his advocacy of a proper treatment of the latter; *Ep.* 47),[81] he never encourages any dissolution of social boundaries or distinctions or any abolition of the right to private property. And as noted, of course, Seneca was himself one of the wealthiest men of the Roman world. When in his ninetieth letter he cites the Second Age, he does so, not because he dreamed of resuscitating the morals and the social organization that it had embodied, but because it enabled him to accentuate what he perceived to be the moral decadence and depravity of his own time (90.40–45). However, this decadence and depravity were a given, in his assessment. They might be censured, but would probably never

80 Cf. Capper, "Reciprocity and the Ethics," 508; Hays, *Luke's Wealth Ethics*, 206–7.

81 Cf. G. Reydams-Schils, *The Roman Stoics: Self, Responsibility, and Affection* (Chicago, IL: University of Chicago Press, 2005), 158–9.

recede. As a result, he conceptualized the lifestyle of the Second Age as exclusively and irretrievably—even if regrettably so—belonging to a golden past.

Seen in this light, Luke's decision to model his portrayal of the first congregation on Seneca's description of the Second Age begins to make sense. As noted, I believe that Luke intended this portrayal to help him solve a problem that arose when he chose to accommodate his ethics in Acts to the predilections of Theophilus. Clearly, the moment he did this, and thus accepted to de facto recant the ethics that he had promoted in his gospel, he opened himself to charges of inconsistency. Such charges, of course, could threaten to undermine his credibility as an author and his authority within the church. I suggest that by depicting the first congregation in the way that he did, i.e., in a way reminiscent of Seneca's description of the Second Age, he was attempting to forestall such charges.

It is often observed that there is a certain verbal similarity between Luke's characterization of the first congregation and the sayings of Jesus in Luke 12:33 and 18:22. In all three cases Luke avails himself of the verb πωλέω ("to sell"; cf. Acts 4:34, 37; 5:1). And in both Acts 4:35 and Luke 18:22 he uses the word διαδίδωμι ("to distribute"), while in Luke 12:33 he applies the shorter form δίδωμι ("to give"). Scholars who notice this generally argue that Luke chose to recycle these words to yield the impression among his readers that life in the first congregation formed a fulfilment of the commandment given by Jesus in the gospel to "renounce all."[82] I find that view compelling, but would like to add to it that by so doing while at the same time shaping his depiction of the first congregation in a manner evocative of Seneca's account of the Second Age he enabled himself to *also* signal that this commandment should be seen as inseparably connected to an idyllic past, which, despite its beauty, was incapable of revival—and therefore without any actual normative value for the believers of his own day. What I propose, in other words, is that Luke designed his description of the first congregation in such a way that enabled him to retroactively, so to speak, "seal off" the radical eth-

82 E.g., Tannehill, *Narrative Unity: Acts*, 45–46; M. A. Co, "The Major Summarities in Acts: Acts 2,42–47; 4,32–35; 5,12–16," *ETL* 68 (1992): 73; Mineshige, *Besitzverzicht und Almosengeben*, 78–9; Hays, *Luke's Wealth Ethics*, 193–4.

ics of possessions that he had promoted in his gospel as applicable to all, including his own audience, and to all times, including his own, in a quasi-mythical past (the time of Jesus and the birth of the church), and so in the remainder of Acts develop a new stance on possessions in tune with the wishes of Theophilus without *seeming* to contradict himself (though, as we have seen, that was precisely what he did).

It is clear that the reading I propose here presumes that Luke was at least loosely familiar with Seneca's thinking (otherwise he could not have consciously patterned his account of the first congregation on his portrayal of the Second Age), and expected his readers, or some of them, to have been so too, or at least capable of being made so (otherwise, evoking his thinking would have been meaningless). This is uncertain, of course, but by no means implausible. Seneca was a well-known figure in his own day and beyond, and we have evidence from a fairly early period of a Christian reception of his literature. Tertullian, most importantly, cites him on several occasions (*De an.* 20.1; 42.2; *De res.* 3.3), once (*De an.* 20.1) even labelling him "our Seneca" (*Seneca noster*), which may or may not imply that he saw him as a Christian, but which certainly indicates that he was not the first member of the church to make reference to him. And evidently the apologist Minucius Felix, whose writings are admittedly difficult to date, was very much at home in his work.[83]

In the introduction to this chapter I raised three questions about Luke's portrayal of the first congregation. (1) Why did he ascribe to it a community of goods? (2) Why did he suggest that it was never restored again after it was disbanded? (3) Why did he allow it to show signs of weakness (cf. 5:1–11; 6:1) prior to the moment of its actual dissolution? I am now in a position to answer these questions. Or in fact, I have already done so. So let me here summarize our findings by briefly rehearsing the answers given. With regards to (2), Luke suggested that the first congregation's community of goods was never restored again because he did not wish to signal that the ethics it had embodied held any normative value. And with regards to (1) and (3), he ascribed to the first congregation a community of goods in the first place and allowed it to show signs

83 For an overview and discussion of the early Christian reception of Seneca see J. Stivala, "The Christian After-Life of Seneca the Younger: The First Four Hundred Years" (Ph.D., Australian National University, 2009).

of weakness prior to its actual disbandment because doing so enabled him to bring together, on the one hand, the radical ethics of his gospel's dominant outlook on possessions and, on the other, Seneca's thinking on the Second Age and thereby subtly relegate those ethics to a distant past and so avoid seeming to contradict himself when in the rest of his work he developed a view of possessions diametrically opposite to them. Thus, in my assessment, as intimated earlier, Acts 1–7 and Acts 8–28 reflect the exact same stance on possessions, although certainly the stories that these segments contain offer descriptions of radically different types of behaviour and radically different types of demands.

Let me conclude this chapter by noting that the reading I have proposed comes fairly close to the one which, following Hays, I have categorized above as the interim solution. Like the proponents of this view, I believe that it is possible to conceive of Luke as rubricizing Jesus' most radical demands (those involving a divestiture of everything) as pertinent and binding only in the past. Yet unlike these interpreters, I propose that he had not intended to do this at the time when he wrote the first of his two works. (In that case, including such passages as 14:12–14 and 19:1–10 in the gospel would have been odd and counter-productive.) The thought of doing so occurred to him only after having completed the first of his instalments, when the need for such a manoeuvre emerged as a result of his decision to adopt a new stance on possessions in the second one, in response to criticism from Theophilus. And when it did, the description of the first congregation became his instrument of choice.

4
Luke and Family

In the previous chapter we analysed Luke's discourse on possessions. In this chapter we examine his stance—or stances—on the institution of the family. Before we can do so, however, we need to begin by acknowledging that any discussion of ancient views of the family, including this one, inevitably runs up against problems of terminology and definition. What was "the family" in ancient Rome; and did what we take the term "family" to imply (most commonly, the nuclear family) form a recognizable social unit for people living in the Roman world? These are questions we need to address—but regrettably may not be able to answer in a fully satisfactory way.[1]

We may begin by reflecting on some linguistic problems. The Latin noun *familia*, which underlies the English word "family" and numerous Western equivalents, and which is commonly given as "family" in modern dictionaries, had a wide currency in the ancient world. It did not, however, describe the same social entity that today the word "family" does for us. As one may gather for instance from the treatment of the term by the jurist Ulpian of the third century CE, the word *familia* was most commonly used to signify the collection of slaves and freedmen attached to an individual person or a married couple. Thus, as R. P. Saller has observed, the term *paterfamilias* did not for the Romans mean "family father," as is otherwise frequently assumed, but rather "estate owner"

1 For general introductions to the topic see, e.g., S. Treggiari, *Roman Marriage:* Iusti Coniuges *from the Time of Cicero to the Time of Ulpian* (Oxford: Clarendon, 1991); S. Dixon, *The Roman Family,* Ancient Society and History (Baltimore: Johns Hopkins University Press, 1992); and H. Moxnes, "What Is Family? Problems in Constructing Early Christian Families," in *Constructing Early Christian Families: Family as Social Reality and Metaphor,* ed. H. Moxnes (London; New York, N.Y.: Routledge, 1997), 13–41.

or indeed "slave owner." Naturally, many *patresfamilias* were as a matter of fact "married with children" and hence also "family fathers" in our sense of the term. But it is important to notice that they did not have to be and that the term *paterfamilias* would never be used to designate that particular aspect of their social identity. Any male who was legally autonomous—*sui iuris*—and in possession of slaves and/or freedmen would count as a *paterfamilias*. Whether or not he had a "family" in our understanding of that word would be immaterial.[2]

The word *familia* could, however, also be used in a way that comes slightly closer to our "family," as a designation of the entire group of people who were subject to the *potestas*, i.e., legal authority, of a *paterfamilias*. By that definition the term would signify not only the *paterfamilias'* slaves and freedmen, but also his children and wife, provided in the latter case that the wife had entered *manus* in connection with their marriage and thus been detached from her father's *potestas* and become subject to that of her husband. By the time of the late republic and the early empire, however, marriage *cum manu* had become of a rarity. Thus, in Luke's day wives would almost never belong to their husbands' *familiae*, even by this broader understanding of the term, whereas the husbands' slaves and freedmen inevitably would. According to a third definition, the word designates all of a person's relatives through the male line of descent (i.e., all of his or her so-called agnatic kin). This definition, however, naturally also excludes the possibility of husband and wife belonging to the same *familia*.

The second Latin term regularly rendered as "family" is *domus*, which is considerably closer to our modern understanding of the notion. *Domus* can mean "house" as a physical structure, but can also refer to the group of people living within a house and/or being legally dependent on that particular *domus' paterfamilias*. Husband, wife, and children would thus normally be taken to belong to the same *domus*, but their *domus* would also be thought to comprise their slaves and freedmen. *Domus* could also be used in the broader sense of a person's extended family and would then signify that person's near and distant relatives through the male and

2 R. P. Saller, "'*Familia, Domus*,' and the Roman Conception of the Family," *Phoenix* 38, no. 4 (1984): 336–55.

female lines of descent. The Greek equivalent οἶκος, which is frequently used throughout the Lucan literature, essentially carries the same set of meanings as its Latin counterpart.[3] Thus, whereas we would normally take the word "family" to refer, in the first place, to the nuclear family, it is clear that the Romans did not have a word to designate that particular entity. The meanings of the words they had for "family" interweave with our concept of it, but never pin it down.

Does this mean that the "nuclear family" (in the sense of the father-mother-children triad) was conceptually unknown to the Romans? That is very difficult to say. Numerous scholars have argued that although the Romans had no word for it, the nuclear family was nevertheless the typical family form in the Roman world and thus that Roman households were, for the most part, made up exclusively of one father, one mother, and their biological and/or adopted children. If that is true, it is possible—even likely, perhaps—that the Romans would have had an idea of the nuclear family, even if they did not have a word for it. The truth of the matter, however, is that we cannot tell with any kind of precision just what the typical Roman family form was. The view of the nuclear family as the norm was pioneered by Saller and B. Shaw in an impressive study of commemorative inscriptions on tombstones in the West, and has since gained a significant following among social historians.[4] A good decade later, however, D. B. Martin submitted the same type of evidence (albeit from another geographical region, Asia Minor) to a different hermeneutical approach and reached the exact opposite conclusion. In his view, commemorative inscriptions suggest, if anything, that extended rather than nuclear families were the norm.[5]

Whether Martin's or Saller and Shaw's analytical method is more defensible may be immaterial, however, for as S. Huebner has shown, commemorative engravings are hardly reliable evidence for Roman

3 Cf. Moxnes, "What Is Family?" 20–21.

4 R. P. Saller and B. Shaw, "Tombstones and Roman Family Relations in the Principate: Civilians, Soldiers and Slaves," *JRS* 74 (1984): 124–56; cf. Treggiari, *Roman Marriage*, 410; E. Champlin, *Final Judgments: Duty and Emotion in Roman Wills, 200 B.C.–A.D. 250* (Berkeley, CA: California University Press, 1991), 103–4.

5 D. B. Martin, "The Construction of the Ancient Family: Methodological Considerations," *JRS* 86 (1996): 40–60.

family structures.[6] Clearly, the most reliable type of evidence we have on this topic are census returns. Such returns, however, survive only from the region of Roman Egypt. And a comparative study of Egyptian census returns and commemorative inscriptions from the same region reveals, Huebner demonstrates, that a match between these different collections of evidence is impossible to obtain, irrespective of one's choice of hermeneutical approach to the latter group of data. Whereas the census returns suggest that "multiple-family households consisting of several married couples together with their offspring" were the norm in Roman Egypt,[7] the epigraphic evidence cannot be manoeuvred to yield that result. Given that census returns have not survived from other Roman regions and that the analysis of commemorative inscriptions does not lead to any reliable conclusions, we really have no way of determining just what type of family structure was typical of non-Egyptian Romans, or whether different family patterns would have been characteristic of different Roman regions. The meagreness of our knowledge is captured by the deliberate vagueness of S. Dixon's statement that it is "acceptable to assert that most Romans lived for most of their lives in nuclear households, but only if we appreciate that this covers a multitude of changes and accommodations over the individual life course and that 'the household' was likely to differ significantly from its modern urban equivalent."[8]

Saller, however, contends that we also have literary evidence of a Roman consciousness of the nuclear family. He points specifically to Cicero's *On Duties* 1.58. In this passage, the philosopher-senator sketches a hierarchy of obligations, which, on Saller's reading, divides as follows: "First comes the husband-wife bond, then the parent-child, and third the bonds of those within the *domus*." According to Saller, this hierarchy suggests "that though the Romans had no word for it,

6 S. Huebner, "Household Composition in the Ancient Mediterranean: What Do We Really Know?" in *A Companion to Families in the Greek and Roman Worlds*, ed. B. Rawson, Blackwell Companions to the Ancient World: Literature and Culture (Chichester; Malden, MA: Wiley-Blackwell, 2011), 73–91.

7 Ibid., 90.

8 Dixon, *Roman Family*, 11; cf. also R. Laurence, "Introduction: From *Oikos* to *Familia*: Looking Forward," in *Families in the Greco-Roman World*, ed. R. Laurence and A. Strömberg, *The Family in Antiquity* (London; New York, N.Y.: Continuum, 2012), 2.

they drew a conceptual circle around the mother-father-children triad and made it the center of primary obligations."[9] Saller's analysis, however, distorts the text. Cicero does operate with a tri-partition of duties, but what he suggests is rather that we are obliged primarily toward our country and parents (*patria et parentes*), secondarily, toward "our children and whole household (*liberi totaque domus*), who look to us alone for their protection," and lastly toward our *propinqui*, which presumably, in the present context, should be interpreted as "kinsmen." Despite Saller's contention, there is no discrete mention of "wife." In all likelihood, Cicero thought of the wife as included in the "household," along with slaves, freedmen, and children, the latter of whom he nevertheless chose to speak of separately, ostensibly for the sake of emphasis. In any case, the passage cannot well be taken to substantiate Saller's argument. If anything, it challenges it.

We may summarize the position as follows: (i) the Romans had no word for our concept of the family; (ii) the words they did have for "the family" could designate a variety of social entities; (iii) it is possible, but remains unproven, that Romans had some form of non-verbalized notion of the nuclear family; and (iv) we do not know just what the typical Roman family type was. Undoubtedly some Romans lived at least parts of their lives in nuclear families, whereas others would have lived with other relatives as well and some even in multi-family households.[10] But the ratios between these forms of organization are unknown, except in Roman Egypt.

This regrettable state of affairs should not, of course, lead us to refrain from examining Luke's discourse on the family. It should, however, induce us to recognize (i) that if we use the term "family" as a category for the father-mother-children triad in connection with ancient material, including Luke's writings, we may be best served using it only as a heuristic tool; (ii) that when Luke mentions believers' parents, wives, children and siblings, as he does for instance in Luke 14:26, we have little way of knowing who or how many of these he imagined to be living with them; and (iii) that when Luke speaks of the households, or οἶκοι,

9 Saller, "*Familia, Domus*," 344, 355.
10 Cf. also K. R. Bradley, *Discovering the Roman Family: Studies in Roman Social History* (New York, N.Y.: Oxford University Press, 1991), 125–55.

of certain individuals, as he does repeatedly particularly in Acts, it is rarely possible to tell, even approximately, how many individuals these οἶκοι should be thought to comprise. We should, however, note that although, apparently, they had no word for it, the Romans could think of the ensemble of parents, spouse, siblings, and children as what we might term a "familial entity." Thus, according to Stobaeus' *Anthology* 4.84.23, when discussing the Stoic notion of οἰκείωσις, the second century thinker Hierocles identified precisely these people, and no one else, as the second conceptual circle around the self (second only, that is, to one's own mind and body). Given that Luke appears to have also thought of this group as somehow forming a delineable entity (cf., e.g., Lk. 14:26), I shall use the word "family" in my analyses of his work for the members of this group.

With these considerations in mind, let us now turn to the actual topic of this chapter. I shall begin by setting a context for Luke's discourse on the family through a brief survey of other early Christian views of the family and family related concerns. Next, I shall analyse Luke's treatments of the family, first in his gospel, then in Acts. And finally, in a third step, I shall seek to explain the differences shown to exist between these works.

The Family in Early Christian Thought

Luke, of course, was far from the only early Christian to debate and discuss the institution of the family. Sex, marriage, and family patterns were major issues of controversy in the formative centuries of the Christian church, and remained so through the Middle Ages and beyond.[11] To be

11 For helpful general surveys see, e.g., E. Castelli, "Virginity and Its Meaning for Women's Sexuality in Early Christianity," *JFSR* 2, no. 1 (1986): 61–88; P. Brown, *The Body and Society: Men, Women, and Sexual Renunciation in Early Christianity*, Lectures on the History of Religions 13 (New York: Columbia University Press, 1988); E. A. Clark, "Antifamilial Tendencies in Ancient Christianity," *Journal of the History of Sexuality* 5, no. 3 (1995): 356–80; C. Osiek and D. L. Balch, *Families in the New Testament World: Households and House Churches*, The Family, Religion, and Culture (Louisville, KY: Westminster John Knox Press, 1997), 103–55; K. L. Gaca, *The Making of Fornication: Eros, Ethics, and Political Reform in Greek Philosophy and Early Christianity*, Hellenistic Culture and Society 40 (Berkeley, CA: University of California Press, 2003); and recently K. Harper, *From Shame to Sin: The Christian*

able to appreciate the contours of Luke's thinking on these matters it will be useful, I believe, to begin this chapter with a brief overview of the dominant perspectives on the subject. The overview does not aim to be exhaustive, only to afford us with enough of a general sense of the leading positions in the ancient church to permit us to grasp the profile(s) of Luke's family discourse.

Given that Paul is our earliest extant source for Christian theology his thoughts on family matters form a natural point of departure. Interestingly, however, Paul's discussions of family issues centre almost exclusively on the question of marriage versus celibacy. Paul had remarkably little to say, for instance, about child-parent relationships. In 1 Corinthians 7:14 he mentions that children of mixed marriages (i.e., marriages between believers and non-believers) are "holy" (ἅγια), not "unclean" (ἀκάθαρτα), and in 5:1–13 we learn that he did not approve of believers sleeping with their fathers' wives. Apart from that, he is silent on the issue. In 1 Corinthians 7, however, he engages in a lengthy discussion of sexual ethics, offering his readers instruction on whether to marry, with all that marriage frequently implies, or remain celibate.

Paul's advice is slightly complicated. As a general rule, he explains, celibacy is preferable. The institution of marriage is part of the fabric of the present world, and "the form of this world is passing away" (7:31). Indeed, "the appointed time has grown very short" (7:29). Furthermore, those who marry take on a wealth of anxieties about "the affairs of this world," including concerns about how to best please their respective marriage partners. Celibates, on the other hand, are free to devote their thoughts to the Lord and may thus concentrate entirely on how to become "holy in body and spirit" (7:32–34). His recommendation of celibacy, however, is not unqualified. His comments in chapter 7 evidently form a response to a query put by the Corinthians about whether it is advisable for a man "to touch" (ἅπτεσθαι) a woman (7:1). From Paul's remarks we may gather that a number of the Corinthians had themselves answered the question in the negative and already decided in one form or another to separate from their

Transformation of Sexual Morality in Late Antiquity, Revealing Antiquity 20 (Cambridge, MA: Harvard University Press, 2013).

spouses and embrace a life of sexual abstinence. It is possible, as Osiek and Balch have argued, that all or some of them had chosen to do so on the basis of a belief, rooted in the medical handbooks of their day, that the act of sexual intercourse implied a loss of bodily πνεῦμα that rendered the spiritual gifts mentioned by Paul in chapters 12–14 harder to obtain.[12] It is also possible that they considered marital intercourse sinful or in some other sense incompatible with the type of devotion they wished to exhibit toward Christ. Whatever their motives, Paul categorically dismisses their approach. Divorce between Christians, he claims, is inadmissible, by command of the Lord (7:10), and even continence between marriage partners ought to be avoided, except possibly on the basis of mutual consent and for limited periods of time (7:2–6). Christians living in mixed marriages might legitimately choose to divorce their partners should the latter wish it so, but they should not, or at least should not feel obliged to, initiate the process themselves (7:12–16).

Paul's insistence that married couples ought not to avoid sexual contact for extended stretches of time was primarily based on an assessment that most people, not least those already attuned to married life, lack the ability to remain continent, and if they try will be likely to succumb to satanic temptation (and pursue erotic fulfilment outside the bounds of wedlock) (7:4–5). The same pessimistic (or optimistic, depending on one's perspective) judgment about the powers of human desire informs his advice to the unmarried, i.e., to the widows and the young. Although he insists that celibacy could well be the best thing for them, he stresses that they should not hesitate to (re)marry, if they sense that the cravings of the flesh are too intense to be kept under control. For, as he states 7:9, "it is better to marry than to burn." It is worth noticing, with Martin, that what Paul condoned was not passionate but rather dispassionate sex between marriage partners. Marital sex was a means precisely to avoid "burning."[13] Paul's discourse in 1 Corinthians 7 reveals that he perceived the choice between marriage and celibacy essentially as an ἀδιάφορον,

12 Osiek and Balch, *Families in the New Testament World*, 104–7.

13 D. B. Martin, "Paul without Passion: On Paul's Rejection of Desire in Sex and Marriage," in *Constructing Early Christian Families: Family as Social Reality and Metaphor*, ed. H. Moxnes (London; New York, N.Y.: Routledge, 1997), 201–15.

an "indifferent," as the Stoics would term it. Opting for the latter might, in some cases, be preferable to the alternative, but on the whole what mattered to him was that believers conducted themselves uprightly in whatever civil status might suit their spiritual habitus.

If Paul was a somewhat hesitant supporter of marriage, regarding it primarily as a "defence against illicit desires,"[14] later New Testament authors, some of whom were writing in his name, warmly embraced the institution and eagerly promoted traditional family mores. The writers of Ephesians, Colossians, and the Pastorals, like the author of 1 Peter, thus all assumed the legitimacy of marriage, even identifying the maintenance of conventional Roman family structures (whatever exactly they were; cf. above) as an inexorable Christian duty (Eph. 5:22–33; 6:1–9; Col. 3:18–22; 4:1; 1 Tim. 2:11–14; 6:1–2; 2 Tim. 3:2; Tit. 2:4, 9; 1 Pet. 2:18–3:7). According to the Pastorals, ecclesial officers should be married, although only once, and capable of controlling their households (τοῦ ἰδίου οἴκου καλῶς προϊστάμενον), including their children. "For if someone does not know how to preside over his own household, how will he attend to the household of God?" (1 Tim. 3:5, cf. 3:1–5, 12; 4:3; Tit. 1:6). In partial conformity with Augustan family legislation,[15] the author also establishes that widows below the age of sixty must remarry, "bear children, and manage their households" (τεκνογονεῖν, οἰκοδεσποτεῖν; 1 Tim. 5:14) and even, which cannot but strike the modern reader as disturbing (if not offensive), that the salvation of female believers will depend on their willingness and capacity to bear children and raise them in accordance with the author's conception of the Christian code of conduct (2:15). By fulfilling the roles of dutifully procreant wives they will atone for their complicity in the fall of Eve (2:13–14).

The notion that sex and the rearing of families should be seen to integrate naturally in the fabric of Christian life is pursued by a number of writers from the second century onwards. In *Vision* 2.2.3, the seer Hermas is instructed by the pre-existent Lady Church to regard his wife for the future merely as a "sister" (cf. ἀδηλφῇ), a commandment that can

14 D. G. Hunter, *Marriage, Celibacy, and Heresy in Ancient Christianity: The Jovinianist Controversy*, Oxford Early Christian Studies (Oxford: Oxford University Press, 2007), 89.

15 See, e.g., Treggiari, *Roman Marriage*, 60–80.

hardly be construed in any other way than to imply that he is to live with her in sexual abstinence.[16] However, in later visions Hermas learns (as do we) that this commandment should be taken to apply to him alone (*Man.* 4.1.1–11) and even that for Christians generally remarriage after the death of a spouse is acceptable, although remaining in a state of widowhood might be more honourable "before the Lord" (*Man.* 4.4.1–2). In a similar vein, in 5:6–7, the author of the *Letter to Diognetus* declares that Christian believers "marry and have children" (γαμοῦσιν ὡς πάντες, τεκνογονοῦσιν) "like everyone else" and in that regard distinguish themselves from pagans only in never choosing to expose any undesired offspring. Likewise Justin Martyr (*1 Ap.* 15:1–8; 29:1–3) and Athenagoras (*Legat.* 33.1–4) inform their audiences that Christians generally marry, but only once and only for the sake of procreation, although both of them also recognize and even pride themselves on the fact that numerous Christian choose to elude marriage out of a desire to "remain pure."

Arguably, Clement of Alexandria offered the early church's most vigorous defense for the institutions of marriage and family. For Clement, the doctrine of the goodness of creation necessarily implied that the act of procreation, as long as it took place within the confines of lawful marriage, had to be agreeable to God. Naturally, to embrace sexual abstinence "in accordance with the norm of health and to combine it with piety, in gratitude for God's gift of grace" could be acceptable (*Misc.* 3.12.79, 88; 18.105.1), but to reject marriage and proscribe the rearing of families was to "blaspheme, with sham piety (εὐφήμως), both the creation and the holy Creator, the almighty only God" (3.6.45.1)—and ironically to set one's hope on the genitalia (3.18.109.3). By contrast, conscientious fathers who preside over their households provide at least a faint imitation of divine Providence (7.11.70.7); even their seed is sacred (3.6.47.1). Clement's veneration for the institution of the family leads him to an astonishing reading of Matthew 18:20, "Who are the two or three who gather in the name of Christ with the Lord in their midst? By three does he not mean husband, wife, and child?" (3.10.68.1–4).[17] Clement, himself

16 Cf. C. Osiek, *Shepherd of Hermas: A Commentary*, Hermeneia (Minneapolis, MN: Fortress Press, 1999), 54–55.

17 Here, perhaps, Clement betrays familiarity with the concept of the nuclear family (cf. above).

perhaps a married man, however, is careful to emphasize that Christians may marry only once and only for the sake of reproduction (3.11.71.4–78.5) and that the legitimacy of sexual intercourse should not be taken as licence for intemperance. Naturally, amatory contact is to be enjoyed only within the bounds of marriage, and even there not passionately, but in the right balanced frame of mind. Husbands ought to feel no desire for their wives, whom they must instead love deferentially. Children must be produced "by a reverent disciplined act of will" (σεμνῷ ... θελήματι) (3.7.52.2; cf. also Tert. *Anim.* 27.4), although elsewhere he assures us that even in the context of marital intercourse there is no harm in "reasoned enjoyment" (τὸ εὐάρεστον μετὰ σωφροσύνης) (3.9.67.1).

Clement's predilection for marriage and the family was shared by numerous later Christians, including Jovinian, Ambrosiaster, Julian of Eclanum,[18] and presumably the silent majority of the church.[19] The rapid growth of Christianity in the early centuries of the movement suggests that the church must have appealed to, and for the most part embraced, people who championed and lived within fully conventional family structures. Yet from its very inception, the Christian mission also encompassed a number of believers who rigorously declined sex and challenged the legitimacy of traditional family patterns. As noted, several members of the Pauline church in Corinth had done so; and in 1 Timothy the author rebukes certain believers, the so-called "false teachers" (ψευδολόγων), for preventing fellow Christians from joining each other in marriage (κωλυόντων γαμεῖν). Likewise, Ignatius of Antioch and the author behind *1 Clement* encountered groups of ascetics, whom both accuse of parading with inappropriate arrogance (*Pol.* 5.2; *1 Clem.* 38.2).

It is difficult to say whether any of these puritans would have perceived sexual abstinence as a requirement for entry into the Kingdom of God. Certainly, from the mid-second century onwards some Christians

18 Cf. D. G. Hunter, "'On the Sin of Adam and Eve': A Little-Known Defense of Marriage and Childbearing by Ambrosiaster," *HTR* 82, no. 3 (1989): 283–99; Clark, "Antifamilial Tendencies," 377–8.

19 K. Cooper, "The Household as a Venue for Religious Conversion: The Case of Christianity," in *A Companion to Families in the Greek and Roman Worlds*, ed. B. Rawson, Blackwell Companions to the Ancient World: Literature and Culture (Chichester; Malden, MA: Wiley-Blackwell, 2010), 192.

did. These Christians are generally labelled as "encratites," partly owing to Irenaeus' treatment of them in the first book of his *Against Heresies*. According to Irenaeus, the fountainhead of all encratite thinking was Tatian, a Syrian pupil of Justin, who, after the latter's death, had "apostatized from the church" and started to preach "that marriage was corruption and fornication" (1.28.1). Irenaeus does tell us from what premises Tatian derived this conclusion. From his own work, however, we can tell that his resentment toward sex and marriage was rooted in a grand theological vision, according to which desire for erotic fulfilment was fundamentally foreign to the true human constitution. On Tatian's understanding, God had shaped the human species in his own divine image (15.1). Initially it had dwelt in the heavenly sphere closely attached to the Holy Spirit ordained for immortality (7.1; 11.2). At one point, however, through the exercise of free will, it detached itself from the spirit and affixed itself to one of God's angels (the devil), "who was more subtle than the rest, having regard to his being the firstborn, and declared him to be God" (φρονιμωτέρῳ παρὰ τοὺς λοιποὺς ὄντι διὰ τὸ πρωτόγονον συνεξηκολούθησαν καὶ θεὸν ἀνέδειξαν) (tr. Ryland, ANF), they were expelled from heaven and fell to the surface of the earth and, ontologically, nearly to the level of mere animals. It was at this moment that the first human beings incurred the desire for sex, and concomitantly the appetite for wealth, power, and glory, having become subject through the fall to the devil and his host of demonic angels (whom Tatian identifies with the members of the Greek pantheon; 8.1–10.3). Their capacity for eternal life, by contrast, they lost. According to Tatian, earthly existence must therefore be conducted as a tightly disciplined endeavour to regain the immortality and the union with the divine that the human species once enjoyed. To succeed in this, one must move beyond the urges that presently unite humanity with the animals, including the desire for sex (cf. Clement *Misc.* 3.12.81–82, 89). And the struggle may be successful. In *Oration to the Greeks* 15.4 he thus rejoices that "for everyone who has been conquered it is possible again to conquer if he or she rejects the condition which leads to death (τοῦ θανάτου τὴν σύστασιν παραιτούμενον)" (tr. Ryland, ANF).

Marcion likewise perceived sex as an obstacle to deliverance. His reasons for doing so, however, differed markedly from those of Tatian. Like most other Christians, he perceived the physical world as an outcome of the demiurgic activity of the god of the Jewish scriptures. Unlike the majority of Christians, however, including Tatian, he regarded this god as an inherently evil deity ontologically inferior to the God of the New Testament and transcendent father of Jesus. Marcion thus declined sex, not because he perceived sexual desire as a tragic outcome of the fall, but because he held that to engage in sex and thus, potentially at least, in the act of reproduction "was to perpetuate a corrupt creation and to fulfil the mandate of the Creator-God 'Increase and multiply.'"[20] For Marcion, to be sexually active was to reinforce and attach oneself to a monstrous world that ought by all possible means to be left behind.

Tatian and Marcion were both from the East, Marcion being the son of a bishop in Sinope in Pontus. Evidently encratite theology flourished particularly in the Eastern Empire.[21] In the late second and early third centuries the Eastern regions gave rise to a body of Christian narratives collectively identified as the *Apocryphal Acts of the Apostles,* which are thoroughly dominated by radically ascetic thought. These narratives unwaveringly describe sexual intercourse, whether marital or not, as filthy (μιαρός) and an object of contempt (κατάγνωσις) (*Act. Andr.* 14; 37; *Act. Thom.* 88), and they feature a rich variety of stories about women who piously break off relations with their (prospective) husbands in the pursuit of a life dedicated to the service of God and unblemished by carnality. The apostles themselves, of course, are celibate and preach sexual abstinence for others as a soteriological requirement (*Act. Andr.* 56; *Acts. Pet. Andr.* 8; 13; *Act. Paul.* 3.5–6, 9; *Act. Pet.* 34; *Act. Thom.* 51; 61; 96; 101; 126). And whereas other early Christians defined the begetting of children as a viable justification for sex, the *Acts* describe it as a just punishment for sexual pleasure (*Acts Thom.* 12; cf. 88)—punishment in the sense that children, as everyone realizes, are lunatics, idiots, and guilty of detestable conduct.

The idealization of celibacy was prevalent in the early church and continent lifestyles grew increasingly popular in the third to the fifth centuries. However, by no means all ascetics shared the perception that sexual

20 Hunter, *Marriage, Celibacy, and Heresy,* 102.
21 Brown, *Body and Society,* 83–102.

abstinence was a Christian obligation and a requirement for deliverance. In 345, at the council in Gangra (in northern Turkey), this understanding was anathematized, and both before and after this date, most ascetically minded writers were able to romanticize sexual abstinence without disparaging, let alone condemning, marriage and marital intercourse.[22] Tertullian, for instance, eulogizes virginity in several of his writings (*Marc.* 1.29.1; *Ux.* 1.2–3; *Exh.* 10.5), but defends the legitimacy of wedlock, though criticizing second marriages (*Exh.* 9), and insisting that nearly insurmountable challenges face those women who give themselves to unbelieving husbands (*Ux.* 2.2–6).[23] John Chrysostom, one of the church's most zealous advocates of puritan practices, readily grants that sex within marriage is not in itself blameworthy (*Hom. 51 Mt.* 5), and that married Christians may gain access to heaven and enjoy the gifts of the Holy Trinity as long as they make use of marriage only with due moderation (*Hom. 7 Hebr.* 4). And Augustine, of course, whose painstaking efforts to subdue erotic desire are so vividly described in the *Confessions*, occasionally speaks of marriage in such acclamatory terms that one cannot help wondering why he did not in the end choose that path for himself (*Conj.* 3.3–7.7; *Nupt.* 1.10.11, 17.19).[24]

For the sake of clarity it is important when analysing the writings of Christian ascetics not to confuse or automatically align aversion to sex with anti-familialism. Naturally, like most Christians presumably, ascetic believers reckoned that one's commitment toward Christ would

22 Clark, "Antifamilial Tendencies," 375–6; Osiek and Balch, *Families in the New Testament World*, 152–5.

23 Over the years, however, and under the mounting influence of Montanism, he grew increasingly hostile to marriage and sex (cf. *Exh.* 9.4 and *Virg.* 10.4).

24 Like many other texts, these passages yield the impression of Christian marriage as a thoroughly virtuous and idyllic partnership. As Clark ("Antifamilial Tendencies," 358; cf. E. A. Clark, *Reading Renunciation: Asceticism and Scripture in Early Christianity* [Princeton, N.J.: Princeton University Press, 1999], 237; C. Osiek, M. Y. MacDonald, and J. H. Tulloch, *A Woman's Place: House Churches in Earliest Christianity* [Minneapolis, MN: Fortress Press, 2006], 148) has noted, numerous other texts, however, testify that the reality of Christian marriages was often rather different, "Letters, sermons, and ecclesiastical decrees constitute an unhappy record of Christian men sleeping with slaves, raping nuns, frequenting brothels, and going to 'sex shows' at which girls swam naked; of Christian women divorcing their husbands; of Christian parents 'leasing' their children into slavery." Clark refers to Aug. *Epp.* 9; 10; 15; *Serm.* 9.3.3; 392.3.2; Jer. *Ep.* 77.3; John Chrys. *Hom. 6 Mt.* 8; *7 Mt.* 6.

need to take precedence over loyalty toward family members. But the adoption of ascetic attitudes did not always imply a rejection of traditional family patterns. Sometimes, admittedly, the two did go hand in hand. E. A. Clark has drawn attention to two fascinating passages in which the passionately ascetic Jerome and John Cassian each engage in startlingly anti-family rhetoric.[25] In *Letter* 39.5.4, the former of these admiringly informs his audience of the reactions of Melania the Elder (at the time, a trusted friend and ally) to the sudden deaths of two of her three sons. These deaths had followed immediately on the death of her husband. But instead of giving herself over to heartache, he writes, she had responded to these deaths with pious gratitude. For, as she had reasoned, by thus liberating her from a "great burden," the Lord had graciously enabled her to serve him more fervently than she had been able to in the past.

The text from John Cassian is even more disturbing. In his *Institutes* 4.27–28 he tells the story of a certain Patermutus, whose commitment, he explains, to "renounce the world" had been of such a formidable nature that he had been able to sever all emotional ties to his eight-year-old son. Patermutus had brought this son with him to the monastery into which he had sought to be admitted. In order to test the level of his dedication, however, the abbot had immediately separated him from his son and dressed the latter in rags instead of clothes and allowed him to be exposed to abuse from the host of other monks. Patermutus, however, had proved himself worthy. For although

> ... the child was treated thus day after day before his eyes, still out of love for Christ and the virtue of obedience the father's heart stood firm and unmoved. For he no longer regarded him as his own son, as he had offered him equally with himself to Christ; nor was he concerned about his present injuries, but rather rejoiced because he saw that they were endured, not without profit; thinking little of his son's tears, but anxious about his own humility and perfection (tr. Gibson, NPNF).

25 Clark, "Antifamilial Tendencies," 357, 65–66.

Later the abbot had told Patermutus that he was annoyed with the child and ordered him to throw him into the river to let him die. At this, Patermutus, "as if this had been commanded him by the Lord, at once snatched up the child, as quickly as possible, and carried him in his arms to the river's bank to throw him in." However, the child survived, to much of his father's surprise; for before giving the order, the abbot had secretly stationed a couple of his monks by the bank of the river to rescue the boy from drowning.

Cassian clearly intended the reader to respond to the father's actions with admiration. Thus, as a conclusion to the story of Patermutus, he notes that his devotion to the divine as revealed through these actions

> ... was so acceptable to God that it was immediately approved by a divine testimony. For it was immediately revealed to the Superior that by this obedience of his he had copied the deed of the patriarch Abraham. And when shortly afterwards the same Abbot of the monastery departed out of this life to Christ, he preferred him to all the brethren, and left him as his successor and as Abbot to the monastery (tr. Gibson, NPNF).

Although Jerome's and Cassian's language is radical, disconcerting perhaps, we should notice that neither of them defines the renunciation of family ties as a precondition for salvation. For them, the actions of Patermutus and Melania were proofs of their exceptional worth, not evidence of attitudes that needed to be emulated by others. Marcion, on the other hand, seems to have held that deliverance would require both an abstention from sexual activity and a detachment from all of one's close biological kin, including any children one might have (Tert. *Marc.* 1.29.1; Epiph. *Pan.* 1.3.42.11.70).[26]

In other cases, however, ascetics were able to embrace, and even prescribe, sexual abstinence without adopting decidedly anti-family attitudes. Numerous ascetics, for instance, chose to retain largely traditional family structures by living in what was termed "spiritual marriages," which is to say partnerships in which Christian men and women

26 Cf. Brown, *Body and Society*, 89.

would live together (sometimes even sharing the same bed) but abstain from sexual intercourse. As Osiek and Balch have noted, this practice often met with suspicion from other puritans (including Jerome, who regarded the arrangement as a front for physical lust), but nevertheless continued well into the Middle Ages.[27] Likewise the authors of the *Apocryphal Acts*, although repeatedly casting the domestic space as a stage for conflict and division, generally imply that conventional family structures can and perhaps ought to be preserved and nurtured as long as they do not constrain believers' commitments to a celibate lifestyle. In the *Acts of Thomas*, for instance, Judas Thomas instructs a newly-wed couple in sexual abstinence, but without in any way encouraging them to separate from each other (12; cf. 131). In the *Acts of John*, our protagonist heals the sons of Antipatros and afterwards orders him to distribute his funds among the poor—but not to leave his sons (56–57).[28] In the *Acts of Paul*, the apostle fasts with a certain Onesiphorus along with the latter's "wife and his children" (3.23). And in the *Acts of Peter* we hear of a young woman who piously accompanies her blind mother into the house of Marcellus (20), and even, in *Cod. Berol.* 8502.4, that Peter himself had a daughter, whom he continued to care for—though admittedly in what most would take as a rather bizarre and gruesome manner, by keeping her partially paralyzed to protect her from exposure to sexual aggression.

As noted, completeness has not been the aim of this survey. I have wished merely to identify the dominant trends in early Christian thinking on family and sexuality, to provide, if only an outline, a context for Luke's discourse on the family. Let us briefly summarize our findings. (i) In the formative centuries of the Christian church the majority of believers appear to have endorsed and conducted their lives within the framework of traditional Roman family structures. (ii) Over the years, particu-

27 Osiek and Balch, *Families in the New Testament World*, 154–5.

28 In the *Apocryphal Acts* the apostles actually never command anyone to leave any of their family members, except for sexually aggressive and inconsiderate husbands. A possible exception is the *Acts of Peter and Andrew* 13, where Peter promises the wealthy Onesiphorus that he will obtain the ability to perform miracles if he agrees to forsake his wife and possessions. Interestingly, however, we never hear that the latter actually leaves or takes steps to leave his wife, although in 20–22 he does promise to renounce his wealth.

larly from the mid-second century onwards, however, a growing number of Christians embraced, encouraged, and in some cases even forcefully prescribed sexual abstinence. Some of these believers also fetishized the notion of a dissolution or renunciation of family ties; but only rarely did Christians define the rejection of family ties as an obligation and a soteriological requirement. Marcion did—if his detractors may be trusted. And so did Luke, as we shall see. At least to begin with.

Luke's Teaching on Family

As in the previous chapter I begin by examining Luke's gospel and then afterwards turn to Acts. But first I want to briefly consider how the family is treated in the works of his predecessors Mark and Matthew (cf. my acceptance of "the Farrer," the "Farrer-Goulder," or the "Luke-Matthew hypothesis" in chapter 1). I do this because Luke develops his teaching on the family in the gospel almost exclusively (if not entirely) through redactional reworkings of material that he inherited from these writers, and, as a result, because I will conduct my examination of his treatment of the family in this volume in a primarily redaction-critical fashion. To that end, a brief clarification of the views of Mark and Matthew will be helpful.

I noted above that the majority of Christians of the early centuries, even among those who did not adopt ascetic practices, believed that in cases of conflict, loyalty toward family members should yield to allegiance to Christ. Mark and Matthew did so, too. And both writers seem to have believed that such conflict was likely to arise. Both of them thus record Jesus' prediction that the future will bring sufferings and situations in which "brother will betray brother to death, and a father his child, and children will rise against parents and have them put to death" (Mk 13:12; Mt. 10:21, slightly different). And Matthew even has Jesus declare that he himself has come not to bring peace to the world, but a sword, "For I have come to set a man against his father, and a daughter against her mother, and a daughter-in-law against her mother-in-law; and one's enemies will be members of one's own household" (10:34–36).

Mark and Matthew clearly imply that Christians must be ready to sacrifice family ties for the sake of Jesus. In both gospels we hear that the disciples leave their families to follow Christ (Mk 1:16–20; 10:28–31; Mt. 4:18–22; 19:27–30) and even that Jesus himself scorns the importance of his own bloodlines (Mk 3:31–35; Mt. 12:46–50). Even so, it would be inaccurate to describe these gospels as distinctly anti-family.[29] Both narratives prohibit divorce (Mk 10:2–12; Mt. 5:31–32; 19:3–9), and Matthew even emphasizes the appropriateness of the fifth commandment of the Decalogue (15:1–9). And while both of them have the disciples leave their families for the sake of following Christ, neither of them defines such conduct as an actual obligation. Thus, what we see in Mark and Matthew is more of a relativization than a rejection of conventional family structures. To the extent that family members or families as collective units form an obstacle to one's commitment to Christ, they must be abandoned or otherwise dismissed. But traditional family patterns are not by themselves incompatible with Christian existence. Matthew, in 10:37, captures the outlook of both, "Whoever loves father or mother more than me (ὑπὲρ ἐμέ) is not worthy of me; and whoever loves son or daughter more than me (ὑπὲρ ἐμέ) is not worthy of me."

With Mark and Matthew and the material analysed in the previous section in the back of our minds, let us now proceed to Luke. At some point in late antiquity, presumably in the early decades of the fourth century, an anonymous author penned what modern scholars have generally agreed to call Luke's anti-Marcionite preface.[30] According to this preface, the writer of the Lucan oeuvre was from Antioch; a physician by profession and a disciple of the apostles, who had followed Paul until the latter's martyrdom; unmarried and childless (ἀγύνως, ἄτεκνος/*uxorem nunquam habuit, filios nunquam procreavit*), and deceased at the age of eighty-four in the region of Boeotia (in Greece). Naturally this is all fiction. Some of the author's information (that Luke was a physician and

29 So also S. C. Barton, *Discipleship and Family Ties in Mark and Matthew*, SNTSMS 80 (Cambridge: Cambridge University Press, 1994).

30 Although its anti-Marcionite character is certainly debatable; cf. J. Regul, *Die antimarcionitischen Evangelienprologe*, Vetus Latina. Die Reste der altlateinischen Bibel. Aus der Geschichte der lateinischen Bibel 6 (Freiburg: Herder, 1969), 197–267.

somehow associated with Paul) derives from the Letter to Philemon (24), in which, however, the apostle almost certainly does not speak about our Luke, and from the ps.-Pauline letters Colossians (4:14) and 2 Timothy (4:11). The rest may be ascribed to a later Christian tradition or, alternatively, the personal imaginings of the "anti-Marcionite" author. However, although neither we, nor the author of the preface, nor the tradition on which he may have relied, have, or had, any knowledge of the biographical details of "the historical Luke," it is unsurprising that at some point in the early centuries of the church the notion would arise that this person did not conduct his life in the company of wife and children. The attitude he expresses in his gospel toward the institution of the family is one of such marked hostility that it is hard to see him in the role of anything even remotely resembling the traditional Roman *pater*.

As noted, I will analyse Luke's treatment of the family in the gospel primarily redaction-critically. A natural place to begin the investigation is Luke's reception in 14:15–24 of Matthew's parable of the wedding banquet in 22:1–14. Everyone agrees that the passages recount essentially the same story, although some obviously hold that Luke had access to it through Q rather than Matthew. Despite the clear similarities, however, Luke's version of the story differs markedly from that of Matthew in ways that can only be taken to reflect a thoroughly hostile stance toward the institution of the family, and marriage in particular. In Matthew's version, Jesus likens the realm of heaven to a king, who organizes a wedding banquet (γάμους) for his son. Those initially invited, however, "paid no attention to it and went away, one to his farm, another to his business, while the rest seized his slaves, maltreated them, and killed them" (22:5) The king responds by ordering them all dead and sending his servants into the streets to summon in their place each and every one they might find. Luke's story departs from Matthew's in various respects. For instance, it omits the troubling detail about the guest not properly dressed and hence bound and thrown out into the outer darkness (Mt. 22:13). For our purposes, however, the most intriguing changes concern the descriptions of the banquet and the reactions of one of those initially invited. Apparently averse to the idea of associating God's kingdom with the institution of marriage, he recasts Matthew's wedding banquet as merely "a great feast" or "supper" (δεῖπνον μέγα) (14:16); and no less significantly he suggests that one of the original invitees excused himself along the following lines, "I have just been married and therefore cannot come (γυναῖκα ἔγημα καὶ διὰ τοῦτο οὐ δύναμαι ἐλθεῖν)" (14:20). Thus, whereas in Matthew's version a wedding features as an image of the heavenly kingdom, in Luke's adaptation of it a wedding, by way of contrast, features as a hindrance to entering it.[31]

The same critical view of marriage informs his redaction of Jesus' ban on divorce in Mark 10:2–12 and Matthew 19:3–9.[32] As noted, in both Mark and Matthew Jesus explicitly forbids the dissolution of marriage, "What God has joined together let no one separate" (Mk 10:9; Mt. 19:6). Matthew's Jesus, to be sure, sanctions divorce in cases of πορνεία. (Indeed, he might be taken to demand it and thus at this point be in line with Augustus' law on adultery, the *Lex Iulia de adulteriis coercendis*.) Both writers, however, describe remarriage after divorce as adultery. Luke retains only this last bit of Mark and Matthew's stories, "Anyone," his Jesus declares, "who divorces his wife and marries another commits adultery, and whoever marries a woman divorced from her husband commits adultery" (16:18). The ban on divorce has dropped out.

Luke 16:18 may thus be taken to suggest that unlike Paul, Mark, and Matthew, Luke approved of divorce, and 18:28–30 confirms this.[33] In these verses Luke performs a similarly telling redaction of Mark 10:28–31 and Matthew 19:27–30. The passage, as we have seen in previous chapters, reports an exchange between Peter and Jesus following on the latter's dialogue with the rich young man, or in Luke's case the rich ruler. According to all three accounts, Peter remarks that he and the other disciples have left everything (πάντα), or in Luke's case "their own" (τὰ ἴδια), for the sake of following him. In Mark and Matthew Jesus responds (here in the wording of Mark), "Truly I tell you, there is no one who has left house or brothers or sisters or mother or father or children or fields, for my sake and for the sake of the good news, who

31 T. K. Seim, *The Double Message: Patterns of Gender in Luke-Acts*, Studies of the New Testament and Its World (Edinburgh: T. & T. Clark, 1994), 225.

32 Cf. also ibid., 224.

33 This is brought out well in B. K. Diderichsen, *Den markianske skilsmisseperikope: Dens genesis og historiske placering* (Copenhagen: Gyldendal, 1962), 52–66. The work is in Danish, but contains a "Zusammenfassung in deutscher Sprache" on pp. 347–54.

will not receive a hundredfold now in this age—houses, brothers and sisters, mothers and children, and fields, with persecutions—and in the age to come eternal life" (10:29–30; cf. Mt. 19:28–29). Interestingly, but in conformity with their joint ban on divorce, neither Mark nor Matthew includes spouses among those whom, according to Jesus, one will be amply remunerated for abandoning. Luke, on the other hand, does, "Truly I tell you, there is no one who has left house or wife (γυναῖκα) or brothers or parents or children, for the sake of the kingdom of God, who will not receive back many times more in this age, and in the age to come eternal life" (18:29–30). Furthermore, he leaves out the detail about regaining a family.

Arguably, Luke's most intriguing redactional choice on the topic of marriage may be found in 20:27–40. Mark 12:18–27 and Matthew 22:23–33 relate the story of Jesus' debate with a group of Sadducees on the topic of the resurrection. Jesus' interlocutors (cunningly) ask him which of seven brothers who had all been married to the same woman (and thus acted in accordance with the notion of "levirate marriage") would be considered her husband in the afterlife. Jesus rejects the question, countering that none among the resuscitated will be "husband" or "wife." "For when they rise from the dead, they neither marry nor are given in marriage, but are like angels in heaven" (Mk 12:25; cf. Mt. 22:30). Luke, however, modifies Jesus' answer in a way that astonishingly transforms the specific condition that Mark and Matthew ascribe to post-resurrection life in heaven into a present earthly reality for those who will be eligible for it. "Jesus said to them, 'Those who belong to this age marry and are given in marriage (οἱ υἱοὶ τοῦ αἰῶνος τούτου γαμοῦσιν καὶ γαμίσκονται); but those who are considered worthy of a place in that age [i.e., the age of the kingdom] and in the resurrection from the dead (οἱ δὲ καταξιωθέντες τοῦ αἰῶνος ἐκείνου τυχεῖν καὶ τῆς ἀναστάσεως τῆς νεκρῶν) neither marry nor are given in marriage. Indeed they cannot die anymore, because they are like angels and are children of God, being children of the resurrection'" (20:34–36). Through this spectacular rewriting Luke classifies celibacy as a precondition for entry into the kingdom.

Some interpreters certainly seek to avoid this conclusion. I. H. Marshall, for example, softens the tone of Luke's discourse. Jesus' response to the Sadducees, he allows, "can be understood to mean the abolition of earthly relationships." It is more likely, however, "that the marriage relationship is transcended in a new level of personal relationships, and the basic point being made is that marriage as a means of procreation is no longer necessary."[34] Bovon grants that, according to a literal reading, the verses proscribe sex and marriage. He quickly adds, however, that it is equally likely that Luke intended either to set up celibacy merely as an ideal toward which one might choose to strive or to imply, along the lines of 1 Corinthians 7:20, that Christians ought to remain in the condition (κλῆσις) in which they were called, and thus that while new marriages should not be contracted, existing marriages should not be dissolved.[35] This last suggestion of Bovon's could have been viable had it not been for 14:26 (to which we shall turn shortly), Luke's general animosity toward marriage, and his decision to displace the ban on divorce in Mark and Matthew. And his first suggestion and that of Marshall are quite unfeasible. As we have seen (chapter 3), Luke nowhere distinguishes between Christian ideals and Christian obligations, and the view that he should have been establishing merely the non-necessity of marriage and childbirth ignores that what Jesus identifies here is a defining condition for those who will participate in the afterlife. His response to the Sadducees can thus hardly be taken in any sense other than as denoting a mutual incompatibility of marriage and enrolment in the Kingdom of Heaven.[36]

In 17:26–37 we detect the same unmistakable acrimony toward marriage, even if the redaction he performs of his *Vorlage* (Mt. 24:36–44) is rather more subtle than what we see in the sections considered above. In 24:36–39 Matthew's Jesus speaks of the Parousia, comparing it to the Flood of Genesis 6–9:

34 Marshall, *Luke*, 741.

35 F. Bovon, *Das Evangelium nach Lukas 4, Lk 19,28–24,53*, EKK 3.4 (Düsseldorf; Neukirchen-Vluyn: Patmos Verlag; Neukirchener Verlag, 2009), 118.

36 Wolter (*Lukasevangelium*, 657) claims that what Luke proscribes is not marriage as such, only "den sexuellen Verkehr zwischen Mann und Frau." One is hard pressed to find such a distinction operative in this or indeed in any passage in Luke.

> But about that day and hour no one knows, neither the angels of heaven, nor the Son, but only the Father. For as the days of Noah were, so will be the coming of the Son of Man. For as in those days before the flood they were eating and drinking, marrying and giving in marriage (τρώγοντες καὶ πίνοντες, γαμοῦντες καὶ γαμίζοντες), until the day Noah entered the ark, and they knew nothing until the flood came and swept them all away, so too will be the coming of the Son of Man.

As Zmijewski and others have noted, Jesus' reference to the days of Noah in this text serves rather exclusively to designate the abruptness and unexpectedness, for most, of the day of the Parousia. Quoting J. Schmid, J. Zmijewski remarks that "mit dem Noebeispiel soll bei Matthäus 'das überraschende unerwartete Kommen des Gerichtstages veranschaulicht werden.'"[37] No critique appears to be intended of the activities (eating, drinking, and marrying) that he ascribes to his own and Noah's generations.

Such a critique, however, is involved in Luke's version of the text.[38] Luke makes two significant changes to Matthew's version both of which point in that direction. First, he substitutes ἐσθίω for τρώγω. As Zmijewski observes, Luke has already used the pair ἐσθίω and πίνω in connection with his parable of the rich fool (in 12:19). The reader can thus hardly avoid conceptualizing the eating and drinking mentioned in 17:27—and hence, by implication, the marrying and getting married away—that apparently characterize each generation as a type of sinful enjoyment that will eventually incur God's wrath. Second, unlike Matthew he likens the day of the Son of Man to another situation described in Genesis, viz., the judgment of Sodom. Roughly like the members of Noah's generation, the Sodomites were "eating and drinking (ἤσθιον, ἔπινον), buying and selling, planting and building" right up to the moment

37 J. Zmijewski, *Die Eschatologiereden des Lukas-Evangeliums: Eine traditions- und redaktionsgeschichtliche Untersuchung zu Lk 21, 5–36 und Lk 17, 20–37* (Bonn: P. Hanstein, 1972), 447–8; cf. J. Schmid, *Das Evangelium nach Matthäus*, RNT 1 (Regensburg: Friedrich Pustet, 1959), 341.

38 Cf. also Seim, *Double Message*, 215.

the catastrophe occurred. By itself this addition need not be significant, although of course the general conduct of the Sodomites hardly featured in the cultural memory of Christianity as particularly worthy. Having pointed to the story of Sodom, however, Luke's Jesus intriguingly enjoins his audience to remember the wife of Lot—μνημονεύετε τῆς γυναικὸς Λώτ! By pointing to her example, Luke should probably be seen as signalling that the pursuits that characterized Noah's contemporaries, the Sodomites, and the members of his own generation—festive eating and drinking, buying and selling, planting and building, *and* marrying and getting married off—are activities that Christians must leave behind, without glancing back, if they wish to avoid a fate like hers.

Marriage was not the only family bond that Luke enjoined his readers to dissolve. We have already seen that he adopts, while supplementing, Mark and Matthew's renderings of Jesus' response to Peter in connection with the dialogue with the rich (young) man, or ruler, a response that stipulates rewards for anyone who leaves siblings, parents, and children behind for the sake of discipleship. In 9:59–62 he strikes a similar chord, at this point even suggesting that leaving family members behind is in fact required for salvation. In 8:18–22 Matthew reports Jesus' response to a disciple *in spe*, who asked for Jesus' permission to bury his father before enlisting in the crowd around him, "Follow me, and let the dead bury their own dead." In 9:59–62 Luke relates the same story, but adds a telling detail about another would-be disciple. This individual approached Jesus proclaiming his wish to follow him with a certain minor proviso: "I will follow you, Lord, but allow me first to say goodbye to those at my home (πρῶτον δὲ ἐπίτρεψόν μοι ἀποτάξασθαι τοῖς ἐπὶ τὸν οἶκόν μου)." Jesus' answer is remorseless, "No one who puts a hand to the plough and looks back is fit for the Kingdom of God." Evidently, according to Luke, leaving one's own family is not merely cause for reward; it is an obligation for anyone who does not wish to fall out on the wrong side of the divide on the day of the Parousia. And the deed must be performed swiftly and abruptly.

Essentially the same lesson may be learned from 14:26. We noted above that Matthew 10:37 may be seen to capture the gist of both Mark and Matthew's discourse on the family, and that this discourse should be seen to convey a relativization of the centrality of family ties.

In 14:26 Luke recasts the Matthean text in a slightly modified form; for him relativization does not quite suffice. Thus, whereas Matthew's Jesus declares that whoever loves his or her father, mother, son, or daughter "more than me (ὑπὲρ ἐμέ) is not worthy of me," Luke's Jesus announces that "Whoever comes to me and does not hate (καὶ οὐ μισεῖ) father and mother, wife,[39] and children, brothers and sisters, yes, and even his own life, cannot be my disciple." It is widely agreed that μισέω should not be construed here in an affective sense. Christians are not being ordered to abhor their wives and kin. The verb, rather, should be taken in its Septuagintal meaning of "reject" or "dismiss" (cf. the Hebrew שָׂנֵא)[40] This may be true, although Luke could hardly expect his audience to fully suppress its ordinary understanding of the word—which normally does hold emotional connotations (cf. LSJ, "μισέω"). In any case, in the light of the passages visited above, it is likely that through his choice of the verb μισέω he intended his readers to perceive Jesus as instructing, even threatening, them and other (would-be) followers of Jesus to break off connections with their households and other close kin.[41] T. K. Seim rightly speaks of Luke insisting that the family members mentioned here need to be "given up."[42]

The texts that we have so far reviewed paint a rather uniform picture of Luke's outlook on family and household, a picture that helps to clarify why Luke's gospel would later become Marcion's biblical book of choice. Marriage and conventional family structures are parts of the present order which for the sake of Christian discipleship and their own future chances of salvation believers must leave behind. A few passages, however, deviate from this pattern. Incidentally, these are the same as those that most conspicuously break with the gospel's dominant outlook on possessions (cf. above chapter 3)—14:12–14 and 19:1–10.

In the former, as we have seen, Jesus informs his wealthy host that he will be counted among the righteous if he agrees to substitute the socially vulnerable for his ordinary dinner guests whenever hosting

39 Notice again how the wife creeps in.

40 E.g., Marshall, *Luke*, 592; Johnson, *Luke*, 229–30; Green, *Luke*, 565; Wolter, *Lukasevangelium*, 516–17.

41 Marshall, *Luke*, 592; Tannehill, *Narrative Unity: Luke*, 138, 222, 252.

42 Seim, *Double Message*, 226.

a banquet. Just as this promise implies that he and others in a similar position will not need to surrender "all," or even any, of their affluence to obtain eternal life, it presumes that he and others may also omit abandoning the members of their households (wives, children, freedmen, slaves, and, in certain cases, extended kin). In the latter, Jesus responds with the following blessing to Zacchaeus' pledge to relinquish half of his possessions and remunerate any he might have defrauded: "Today salvation has come to this house (τῷ οἴκῳ τούτῳ), because he too is a son of Abraham" (19:9).[43] Neither here nor in 19:5, where Jesus expresses his wish to lodge in the tax collector's house, does Luke affirm that any family members or other dependants should be living with Zacchaeus. But given his social station we should hardly imagine him to be living alone. Thus, in 19:9 Luke should almost certainly be seen as conveying that both Zacchaeus *and* the members of his household were being blessed without any of them being simultaneously ordered to separate from each other as either a result of or precondition for the blessing.[44]

Let us now turn to Luke's second volume. Against the background of the anti-family bent of Luke's gospel (14:12–14 and 19:1–10 notwithstanding), Luke's discourse on family matters in Acts is astonishing. Initially, perhaps, he might be seen to continue the line of the gospel through his characterization of the early Jerusalem community (Acts 2:42–47; 4:23–5:11; 6:1–7). Just as the members of this congregation relinquished all of their possessions for the sake of the common good, they also lived together in ways that appear at least to have softened marriage bonds and definitely stretched traditional family mores. Luke's discourse, however, seems to presume (*contra* Jesus' numerous instruc-

43 Cf. D. L. Matson, *Household Conversion Narratives in Acts: Pattern and Interpretation*, JSNTsup 123 (Sheffield: Sheffield Academic Press, 1996), 70–75.

44 One might possibly also point to Lk. 12:51–53 as a slightly aberrant text. Although in this passage Luke's Jesus clearly speaks of household division as a result of the advent of Christianity, he could be seen to be tacitly suggesting that "alliances" between individual members of segregating households may endure and thus that members of what was once the same family may, in one form or another, legitimately remain together even after having joined the Christian movement. In any case, however, Luke's emphasis in this section clearly lies on Christianity's divisive effect on households.

tions) that family members were not commanded to separate. Whatever the nature of their guilt (cf. above chapter 3), Ananias and Sapphira were not condemned for remaining together as a couple.

Irrespective of how, exactly, traditional family structures should be seen to have been shuffled during the "Jerusalem springtime," it is clear—if surprising—that none of Luke's anti-family rhetoric survives the dissolution of the *Urgemeinde* in 8:1. From this moment on, not a single believer, or prospective believer, is reported by Luke to have abandoned his or her household, or any member of it, either for the sake of "the Way" or any other reason. Neither is anyone encouraged, let alone commanded, to do so. On the contrary, numerous passages in Acts 8–28 suggest that Christianity should be seen very much as a "family affair." In 20:20 Paul declares before the Ephesian elders to have preached the gospel to them κατ᾽ οἴκους. But unlike in the gospel, Christian teaching is no longer seen as dissolving households. In chapter 18 we meet the married couple Priscilla and Aquila, who become Paul's travelling partners, and whose missionary efforts (18:26) are recognized and implicitly applauded.[45] Nothing suggests that they divorced each other or indeed ought to have done so. Similarly, Luke recounts the conversions of no fewer than four households,[46] nowhere suggesting that the members of these οἶκοι did not remain together: in Acts 10 Peter converts the household of Cornelius (cf. the wording of Peter's report in 11:14, ὃς λαλήσει ῥήματα πρὸς σὲ ἐν οἷς σωθήσῃ σὺ καὶ πᾶς ὁ οἶκός σου); in 16:15 we hear of Paul's conversion of Lydia and her οἶκος, "When she and her household were baptized (ὡς δὲ ἐβαπτίσθη καὶ ὁ οἶκος αὐτῆς), she urged us," etc.; and 16:30–34 Luke tells us the story of the conversion of the Philippian prison guard. His emphasis on the role of the household in this passage is remarkable:

45 M. R. D'Angelo ("'Knowing How to Preside over His Own Household': Imperial Masculinity and Christian Asceticism in the Pastorals, Hermas, and Luke-Acts," *Semeia* 45 [2003]: 282) speculates whether Luke might have understood the couple to have lived together celibately. Even if he did, however, they would hardly have qualified as "sons of resurrection," as she presumes, according to the definition of Lk. 20:36, since there it is marriage and not merely marital intercourse that precludes participation in the afterlife.

46 Cf., above all, Matson, *Household Conversion Narratives.*

> And he brought them outside and said, "Sirs, what must I do to be saved?" They answered, "Believe in the Lord Jesus, and you will be saved, you and your household (σὺ καὶ ὁ οἶκός σου)." They spoke the word of the Lord to him and to all who were in his house (σὺν πᾶσιν τοῖς ἐν τῇ οἰκίᾳ αὐτοῦ). At the same hour of the night he took them and washed their wounds; then he and his entire family were immediately baptized (καὶ ἐβαπτίσθη αὐτὸς καὶ οἱ αὐτοῦ πάντες παραχρῆμα). He brought them up into the house and set food before them; and he and his entire household rejoiced that he had become a believer in God (καὶ ἠγαλλιάσατο πανοικεὶ πεπιστευκὼς τῷ θεῷ).

Lastly, 18:8 recounts how "Crispus, the official of the synagogue, became a believer in the Lord, together with his whole household (σὺν ὅλῳ τῷ οἴκῳ αὐτοῦ)." Texts such as 1 Corinthians 7:12–16, 21–24; and 1 Peter 3:1 inform us, in the words of Osiek, M. Y. MacDonald, and J. H. Tulloch that historically "subordinate members of households" were not always converted along with the senior member(s).[47] Acts, however, paints an idealized picture, according to which households would never become merely "partly Christian." Subordinates unquestioningly, yet apparently enthusiastically, follow the lead of their household heads. In 12:11–17, even the παιδίσκη of Mary, mother of John Mark, features as a firm, and passionate, believer, "And when he [i.e., Peter] knocked at the door of the gateway, a slave girl named Rhoda came to answer. Recognizing Peter's voice, in her joy she did not open the gate (καὶ ἐπιγνοῦσα τὴν φωνὴν τοῦ Πέτρου ἀπὸ τῆς χαρᾶς οὐκ ἤνοιξεν τὸν πυλῶνα) but ran in and reported that Peter was standing at the gate" (12:13–14).

Reading through Luke's discourse on the family in Acts 8–28 one almost hesitates to believe that these chapters were penned by the same author who had previously written such passages as Luke 9:59–62 and 20:27–40. There is only one verse in this large body of text that might conceivably be seen to continue the gospel's anti-family program. And even here we should proceed with care. In Acts 24:25 we learn that when summoned by the governor Felix, in the company of his wife Drusilla,

47 Osiek, MacDonald, and Tulloch, *Woman's Place*, 158.

to inform him further "about the faith in Christ Jesus,"[48] Paul started to preach about "justice, ἐγκρατείας, and the coming judgment." At its most basic level, the noun ἐγκράτεια, featuring here in the genitive, means "mastery" or "control." In ethical discourse it would frequently serve to designate *self*-mastery, or more narrowly the mastery of one's sexual appetites. And in certain branches of Christian literature of the second century onwards it evolved into a *terminus technicus* for complete and permanent sexual abstinence (cf. the concept "encratism" discussed above). Theoretically one could propose, as indeed Seim has done, that Luke applies the noun here in accordance with this later Christian usage of the term and thus presents Paul in 24:25 as a preacher of celibacy.[49] On such a reading Luke could be taken, at this particular moment, to be challenging the legitimacy of traditional household organization, resuming the anti-family discourse of his gospel.

Luke's intentions were presumably rather different, however. As most scholars recognize, Luke should probably be seen in this passage as engaging in a little satire.[50] To appreciate the author's wit we should recognize that, as a Roman, Felix would probably have taken ἐγκράτεια to designate not celibacy, which Romans rarely viewed as a virtue except in very young women and certain cultic officials like the Vestal priestesses,[51] but rather, like its Latin near-equivalent *continentia*,[52] respect for sexual boundaries, including above all the respect for the boundaries around other men's marriages.[53] It appears to have been generally recognized in antiquity that Felix himself had not exhibited such respect. According

48 According to 24:22, the governor was already well-informed about "the Way."

49 Seim, *Double Message*, 198; cf. also 208.

50 E.g., H. Conzelmann, *Acts of the Apostles: A Commentary on the Acts of the Apostles*, Hermeneia (Philadelphia: Fortress Press, 1987), 201; Johnson, *Acts*, 418; Mason, *Josephus and the New Testament*, 176–7; Pervo, *Acts*, 603–5.

51 Cf., e.g., R. Langlands, *Sexual Morality in Ancient Rome* (Cambridge: Cambridge University Press, 2006).

52 Cf. Edwards, *Politics of Immorality*, 81–84.

53 C. A. Williams, *Roman Homosexuality*, 2nd ed. (Oxford; New York, N.Y.: Oxford University Press, 2010), 113–15. Roman morality conceptualized adultery as the most heinous of sexual crimes. In 18 B.C. it became subject to criminal law through the passing of the *Lex Iulia de adulteriis coercendis*. As social historians have shown (cf. Edwards, *Politics of Immorality*, 47–49; Langlands, *Sexual Morality*, 281–363), accusations of adultery were stock material in Roman political invective (e.g., Cic. *Cat.* 2.23; *Phil.* 2.99; Suet. *Aug.* 69; Plut. *Pomp.* 2.4–5; Dio 46.18.3–6).

to Josephus (*A.J.* 20.141–144), Felix's wife Drusilla, who was also the daughter of Agrippa I and sister of Agrippa II, had originally been married to King Azizus of Emesa, who had allowed himself to be circumcised in order to secure the marriage. Obsessed with her beauty, which allegedly exceeded that of all others, Felix had enticed Drusilla through promises and deceit to abandon Azizus and marry him instead. Thus, in a display of anything but self-mastery or ἐγκράτεια, Felix had indulged his illicit sexual cravings and shamefully trespassed on another man's wife. Luke appears to attract his readers' attention to this story by allowing Drusilla to be present during Felix's conversation with Paul and by emphasizing her marriage with the governor (τῇ ἰδίᾳ γυναικί) and her Jewish origin (Ἰουδαίᾳ). Paul's mention of ἐγκράτεια in this verse thus reads like a couched criticism of Felix's morals, and Luke's depiction of the governor's reaction to his preaching—"Felix became frightened and said, 'Go away for the present; when I find time, I will summon you'" (24:25)—as a touch of sardonic irony. Suddenly the dreaded Felix was himself struck with anxiety, seeing that through his lack of self-mastery he might have incurred the judgment from heaven of which the missionary speaks. When seen in this light, it is clear that 24:25 does not, after all, promote celibacy and contest the legitimacy of the family institution. Quite the opposite, it serves to scorn a man who had failed to treat the family of another with due reverence.

Toward an explanation

This survey has revealed a remarkable level of contradiction in Luke's rhetoric on the family. In the gospel we find a wealth of passages that call out for a break with conventional family structures. Believers, in short, are urged to disown their family members, and marriage in particular is classified as an obstacle to salvation. In the history of early Christian thought this approach is paralleled in severity only by such radical thinkers as Marcion. Even the writers of the *Apocryphal Acts of the Apostles* come out as more lenient. A few passages, however, deviate from this perspective, suggesting the acceptability of traditional family organization. Moving into Acts, we initially find the disciples living together in the Jerusalem community in a way that departs from typical household patterns, thus at least partly practising what Jesus had preached, although any actual disbanding of marriage bonds does not appear to have been mandatory, or even encouraged. From the time of the dissolution of the primitive church, however, it is remarkable that we come across not a single adherent of the Christian movement who acts as Jesus had commanded. No one abandons his or her household, and no one urges or advises others to do so. On the contrary, we hear of married believers who together disseminate the word of salvation, and of a series of no fewer than four conversions of entire households, where the members apparently, and clearly justifiably, remain together after their calling. In chapters 8–28 Christianity features frequently as a joint "family commitment" much in the manner of traditional Roman religion, we may note;[54] and far from criticizing the institution of marriage, Luke at one point censures a Roman official for having infringed upon and dissolved the family of another. The Luke of Acts, in other words, suddenly appears close to such thinkers as Clement of Alexandria.

How may this development be explained? Remarkably, the question raised here is frequently left unanswered, and even unexplored. Whereas the polyphony in Luke's discourse on material possessions has attracted keen scholarly interest, as we saw in the previous chapter, commentators have tended to ignore the discrepancies in his language on the household. Seim, for instance, skillfully expounds the anti-familialism of Luke's gospel, but neglects the theological "rehabilitation" of the household in Acts 8–28.[55] Similarly, Osiek and Balch remark that Luke extends a "radical critique of marriage and promotes ascetic values," which is certainly a fair assessment of the Luke of the gospel, but hardly of Acts 8–28, to whom they devote little attention.[56] From a different angle, J. N. Elliott remarks that "[i]n Luke-Acts the household emerges as the preeminent sphere and symbol of the reception of the gospel, Christian identity, and solidarity in the Spirit," without anywhere, however, discussing how

54 Cf. J. M. G Barclay, "The Family as Bearer of Religion in Judaism and Early Christianity," in *Constructing Early Christian Families: Family as Social Reality and Metaphor*, ed. H. Moxnes (London; New York, N.Y.: Routledge, 1997), 66–80; Osiek and Balch, *Families in the New Testament World*, 82–87.

55 Seim, *Double Message*.

56 Osiek and Balch, *Families in the New Testament World*, 143, cf. 136.

such an assessment might cohere with the clear denunciation of the family that we find scattered throughout the gospel.[57] In a similar vein, D. L. Matson explores the centrality of the theme of "household conversion" in Acts, yet without seeking to relate this theme to Luke's rejection of the legitimacy of the household in the gospel.[58] In a series of articles M. R. D'Angelo comments on both some of the passages in which Luke appears to replicate traditional Roman family values and some of those of which the opposite is true.[59] She never sets out to explain the incongruity, however. Lastly, we may mention the recent monograph by W. R. G. Loader on the treatment of sexuality in the New Testament, in which he comments on some of the ascetic material in Luke, but has nearly nothing to say about Acts.[60]

Naturally, to explain the inconsistencies in Luke's rhetoric one could try to recycle the models (interim, bi-vocational, personalist, or symbolic) that have previously been used to make sense of the discrepancies in his teaching on wealth (cf. above chapter 3). However, we have already seen that these approaches are inadequate to explain the properties of Luke's text. We need something different. May our theory about Luke and Theophilus be able to help us out? I believe so. Let me elaborate.

57 J. N. Elliott, "Temple versus Household in Luke-Acts: A Contrast in Social Institutions," in *The Social World of Luke-Acts: Models for Interpretation*, ed. J. H. Neyrey (Peabody, MS: Hendrickson Publishers, 1991), 230.

58 Matson, *Household Conversion Narratives*. Matson in fact suggests that Luke and Acts concur on the topic of the household, and that the emphasis in Acts on households as the pivotal *locus* of conversion is prepared for by Lk. 10:1–12 and 19:1–10. His reference to 19:1–10 is reasonable (cf. above); his invocation of 10:1–12, however, is somewhat strained. Nothing suggests that the homes that the seventy(-two) are instructed to dwell in while they are away should play a central role in their missionary activity. On the contrary, Jesus' direction that they should not "keep moving from house to house" (10:7) suggests that these houses should serve a merely practical purpose and that the missionaries' sermonizing take place in the open (otherwise their preaching would certainly reach a very limited audience).

59 M. R. D'Angelo, "Women in Luke-Acts: A Redactional View," *JBL* 109, no. 3 (1990): 441–61; M. R. D'Angelo, "The ANHP Question in Luke-Acts: Imperial Masculinity and the Deployment of Women in the Early Second Century," in *A Feminist Companion to Luke*, ed. A. J. Levine (London: Sheffield Academic Press, 2002), 44–69; "Knowing How to Preside."

60 W. R. G. Loader, *The New Testament on Sexuality*, Attitudes towards Sexuality in Judaism and Christianity in the Hellenistic Greco-Roman Era (Grand Rapids, MI: Eerdmans, 2012).

It is one of the merits of feminist scholarship to have clarified the ways in which ascetic Christian discourse—for instance, of the sort that we find in Luke's gospel, though that particular text, as we have seen, is rather more radical than most—is likely to have enticed women in the Roman world. We noted in the introduction to this chapter that by the time of the Principate marriage *cum manu*, i.e., marriage in which the wife would enter the *potestas* of her husband, had grown rare. Undoubtedly, this development had increased the level of social freedom and security for Roman wives. Rather than being forced, potentially at least, to submit unconditionally to the will of their husbands, they could now count on the continual protection of their fathers, who remained their legal guardians, and furthermore, on the latter's deaths, inherit and on certain conditions become *sui iuris*. Wives in marriages without *manus* even had the right to initiate divorce,[61] although presumably few will have done so without consulting their own families. One imagines that the mere possibility of one day facing a claim for divorce—and a concomitant repayment of the dowry—is likely to have put a check on at least some husbands' exertion of power.

Even so, the scope of the social roles available to most women remained fairly narrow. Few Romans argued for the appropriateness of female education. The Stoic Musonius Rufus stands as a lone voice (*Disc.* 3). And many sources suggest that women would often have to settle for a life largely secluded from the public arena and in the shadow of their husbands. Dio Chrysostom repeatedly stresses that women are weak, must remain indoors and concern themselves exclusively with household duties (*Or.* 3.70; 7.114; 35:15). Plutarch strikes a similar note. Wives should be adorned with modesty (not expensive clothes), refrain from speaking except through their husbands, and always follow their husbands' moods.[62] Pliny's boast of the virtues of his third wife Calpurnia yields a fine illustration of how Roman males habitually conceptualized proper wifely demeanour:

61 Treggiari, *Roman Marriage*, 28–36.

62 They should even feel honoured, he adds, whenever their husbands would choose to satisfy their desires in the company of other women (*Praec.* 16; cf. also 10, 14–15, 29–32, 48); cf. Osiek and Balch, *Families in the New Testament World*, 63.

> She is highly intelligent and a careful housewife and her devotion to me is a sure indication of her virtue. In addition, this love has given her an interest in literature. She keeps copies of my work to read again and again and even learn by heart. She is so anxious when she knows that I am going to plead in court and so happy when all is over. (She arranges to be kept informed of the sort of reception and applause I receive, and what verdict I win in the case.) If I am giving a reading, she sits behind a curtain nearby and greedily drinks in every word of appreciation. She has even set my verses to music and sings them, to the accompaniment of her lyre, with no musician to teach her but the best of masters, love (*Ep.* 4.19; tr. Radice, LCL).

Another such illustration can be found in Livy's portrayal of the mythically honourable Lucretia (1.57.6–10), whom her husband, Tarquinius Collatinus, and his drinking friends (one of whom will later rape her), find "sitting in the middle of the building among her slave girls working by lamplight, working the wool late into the night" when they walk in on her unannounced.[63]

Osiek and Balch rightly caution us against mistaking admonitions and formalized portrayals by male authors for reliable descriptions of how Roman women actually conducted and experienced their lives.[64] For one thing, the distinction between reality and representation should always be kept firmly in mind; for another, the rhetoric of Livy, Pliny, Dio, and Plutarch presupposes that only a few women truly lived up to the "ideal" they celebrated. Furthermore, we may note that several writers speak (in an equally stylized manner, to be sure) of women who eclipse—and de facto emasculate—their husbands, just as we know that some married women acted as patrons apparently independently of their spouses. Even so, the sources cited here, in addition to a wealth of others,[65] may well be taken to testify to a complex of social expectations that many women,

63 Tr. Langlands, *Sexual Morality*, 86.
64 Osiek and Balch, *Families in the New Testament World*, 63.
65 Many can be found in a recent source, Langlands, *Sexual Morality*.

one presumes, will have been unable to entirely shake off.[66] Seen in this light, the apparent appeal of ascetic Christianity to several women in the Roman world is easily understood. Although it certainly far from always afforded them positions of actual leadership in the church, it nevertheless extended to them, in the words of Seim, "the possibility of a power and an authority from which they were otherwise excluded, and an opportunity to move outside the limiting constraints of the conventional gender-determined roles as daughter, wife and mother."[67]

Among Roman males, on the other hand, at least among those of the comfortable classes, ascetic and anti-family rhetoric of the sort that we find in Luke's gospel could rarely expect to attain a favourable hearing. The passing of Augustus' family legislation (above all the *Lex Julia de maritandis ordinibus* and the *Lex Papia Poppaea*) and the occasional comments by letter writers and historians (e.g., Plin. *Epp.* 1.8.10–11; 4.15.3; Tac. *Ann.* 3.28.6; Dio 56.3.3–5) suggest that Roman men particularly of the upper classes would frequently require some form of legal or moral encouragement to take on marriage and, in the words of Pliny (*Ep.* 1.8.11), "the tedium and hard work involved in bringing up children" (tr. Radice, LCL).[68] Yet apart from a very select group of predominantly Cynic philosophers,[69] and of course some of the Christians mentioned above (especially Marcion), practically no Roman males of whom we have any knowledge appear to have felt even tempted to go to such lengths as to renounce all family ties (in addition to the prospect of a future marriage) to the extent that Luke initially advocated. By the time

66 Osiek and Balch (*Families in the New Testament World*, 58–64) propose that women of the lower levels of society probably enjoyed a higher degree of social autonomy than those in the propertied classes did. This is possible, although our knowledge of the lives of the *humiliores* is too scant to warrant firm conclusions. In any case, Augustine's commendation of his mother's patience with her husband Patrick in *Confessions* 9.9.19 is sadly illuminating of the oppression that "ordinary" Roman wives would sometimes have to endure.

67 Seim, *Double Message*, 220–1; cf. also V. Burrus, *Chastity as Autonomy: Women in the Stories of the Apocryphal Acts*, Studies in Women and Religion 13 (Lewiston, N.Y.: E. Mellen Press, 1987); Castelli, "Virginity and Its Meaning."

68 Cf. Treggiari, *Roman Marriage*, 77–80; S. Dixon, "The Sentimental Ideal of the Roman Family," in *Marriage, Divorce, and Children in Ancient Rome*, ed. B. Rawson (Oxford: Clarendon, 1991), 100.

69 Cf. Barton, *Discipleship and Family Ties*, 47–56.

of the Principate (despite their partially ascetic intellectual heritage) even Stoic philosophers had come to embrace rather traditional types of family life;[70] and traditional Roman family values were, of course, widely celebrated in the Roman world in a wealth of media from tombstones to funerary and forensic oratory to poetry and moral philosophy.[71] This apparent lack of enthusiasm for ascetic and anti-family regimes on the part of at least most upper class males is unsurprising, of course, seeing that the dynamics of the family institution offered to them a social scaffolding for the attainment, preservation, and exertion of status, honour, power, and wealth, just as the very same dynamics, as we have seen, would frequently restrict the freedom of women.

It is worth noting that besides feeling personally unattracted to Luke's anti-family programme, numerous Roman men would presumably also deem it unpatriotic. We noted above that for Paul the purpose of marriage was essentially the—controlled and non-excessive—fulfilment of sexual desire. Roman authors tended to see things otherwise. Although the sources that survive (e.g., Catull. 61) present us with the occasional celebration of marital sensual joy,[72] Roman males in the main considered marriage an unnecessary frame for the attainment of sexual pleasure, which could just as easily, and unproblematically, be achieved by both married and unmarried men in the company of slaves and prostitutes.[73] For Roman men, the objective of marriage was predominantly the production and rearing of children.[74] And although the fulfilment of this purpose would often satisfy personal needs of both an emotional

70 Reydams-Schils, *Roman Stoics*, 143–76.

71 See, e.g., Dixon, "Sentimental Ideal."

72 S. Dixon, "Sex and the Married Woman in Ancient Rome," in *Early Christian Families in Context: An Interdisciplinary Dialogue*, ed. D. L. Balch and C. Osiek, Religion, Marriage, and Family Series (Grand Rapids, MI: Eerdmans, 2003), 111–29.

73 Williams, *Roman Homosexuality*, 50–59. Catullus, in the poem referenced, suggests that male infidelity would often reflect an insufficient level of marital commitment on the part of the wife, "Bride, you too must be careful not to deny what your husband will seek from you, lest he go to seek it from some other source" (61.144–146; tr. ibid., 57). In contrast, female infidelity was socially unaccepted and severely punished; cf., in addition to Williams, Edwards, *Politics of Immorality*, 34–62; T. A. J. McGinn, *Prostitution, Sexuality, and the Law in Ancient Rome* (New York, N.Y.: Oxford University Press, 1998), 140–247.

74 Treggiari, *Roman Marriage*, 5–13.

and a social character, the production of children was also widely perceived as an obligation to the state, whose welfare, social stability, and military strength depended on the continual replenishment of the citizen body (Hierocl. ap. Stob. *Anth.* 4.75.14; cf. 4.67.21; Mus. Ruf. *Disc.* 14; Gell. 1.6.6). So although, as we have seen (cf. above chapter 2), Luke exerted himself to establish the political harmlessness of the church, it is likely that Roman upper-class males (among others) would construe his gospel's discourse on the family in a totally different way.

If the profile I have sketched of Theophilus—as a recent convert and a member of the leisured classes, invested with the Roman aristocratic ideology and intent on sustaining his social position—holds true, it is therefore plausible that he would have responded to Luke's gospel's rhetoric on the family disapprovingly. We are thus able to apply to the present facts the explanatory model that we have developed in the earlier chapters. When setting out to compose his gospel, Luke intended, among other things, to encourage Theophilus to perform a radically ascetic change of life, involving, not only a renunciation of his wealth, but also a radical breach with his family. To achieve this he portrayed such a breach repeatedly as a soteriological requirement. However, realizing both that Theophilus might not be easily convinced and that he himself was not quite prepared to risk losing him as a convert, he included a few passages that left the door open for traditional household organization and lifestyle as a defensible part of Christian existence. And Theophilus, as it turned out, could not be convinced. Thus, in Acts we find Luke embracing traditional family norms, and even celebrating the institution of the household, in the words of Elliott, as precisely "the preeminent sphere and symbol of the reception of the gospel, Christian identity, and solidarity in the Spirit." Up until the moment of the dissolution of the Jerusalem church, he maintains a certain level of continuity with the ascetic strands of his gospel, but only—as follows from our treatment of the *Urgemeinde* in chapter 3—because doing so allowed him in the rest of the narrative to espouse a new and more lenient set of ethical standards without appearing to contradict himself.

5
Conclusion

In this concluding chapter, I want to bring the study to a close by offering a summary of each of its previous chapters and afterwards briefly returning to the discussion about the unity of Luke's writings that I touched upon at the beginning of the book and clarify how the readings that I have proposed may be seen to have contributed to it.

Summary

In chapter 1 I opened the book by placing the discussion in the context of the current debate about the unity of Luke and Acts. Then I offered a sketch of the interpretation of these works that it was going to put forward and examined a number of preliminary questions. The chapter covered a variety of issues, but focused on articulating two propositions. First, it suggested that Luke's attitude to possessions and the institution of the family developed throughout his work from an ascetic position in the gospel to a "bourgeois" position in Acts. Second, it suggested that this development may be explained through a theory about Luke and Theophilus (his dedicatee in both works), which it then went on to delineate. The theory proposed that at the moment of the composition of the gospel Theophilus had been a socially advanced gentile, who had recently adopted the Christian faith and in connection therewith assumed a patron-like function vis-à-vis Luke's community; that through the composition of his gospel Luke had attempted, on the one hand, to strengthen Theophilus' ties to the church by offering him a description of its relationship to Rome, novelty, and the Jews that could be expected to match his ideological presumptions, but also, on the other hand, to persuade him to relinquish his privileged lifestyle in favour of an essentially ascetic form of living; and finally that once Theophilus had read this work (or, alternatively, had had it read to him), he had reacted strongly against this call and in the period that followed convinced Luke to compose his second work—the Acts of the Apostles, which Luke had already planned for—in a way that would authorize rather than, like the gospel, challenge his right to maintain the lifestyle that he was used to. Theophilus, however, had had no quarrels with his outlook on Rome, novelty, and the Jews. Hence, when writing the Acts of the Apostles Luke had maintained the line taken in the gospel on these various subjects. I finally noted that a certain minority of texts in the gospel deviate from its otherwise ascetic ethical stance, and that the presence of these passages naturally requires an explanation.

In chapter 2 I elaborated on the proposal that through the gospel, and Acts, Luke had attempted to strengthen Theophilus' ties to the church by offering him a vision of its relationship to Rome, novelty, and the Jews that could be expected to resonate with his ideological biases. I did this, on the one hand, by demonstrating that in both the gospel and Acts Luke meticulously emphasized the political innocence of the church and carefully dissociated it from the notion of novelty, while at the same time portraying its relationship to the Jews in a way that revealed both its political innocence and its non-novelty. On the other hand, I showed that socially privileged Romans, such as Theophilus, according to the theory presented in chapter 1, were generally very suspicious of both political insubordination and things considered new. Bringing these lines of argument together, I concluded that it therefore makes sense to interpret Luke's discourse on Rome, novelty, and the Jews as revealing an ambition on his part to render the Christian faith more attractive to Theophilus than it might otherwise have seemed, and hence as an attempt to strengthen Theophilus' attachment to the Christian community.

In chapter 3 I examined Luke's discourse on possessions. I did so aiming to demonstrate that Luke's stance on this topic developed as described in chapter 1 and that this development is explicable through the theory about Luke and Theophilus that I delineated there. I opened the chapter by analysing Luke's attitude to possessions in the gospel. I argued that most of the passages there dealing with that issue suggest that material wealth is incompatible with salvation and that believers to be redeemed must renounce *nearly* all of their belongings for the benefit of the poor and even after having done so continue to give alms. I also noted that a few passages deviate from this view by indicating that a more modest level of self-sacrifice and commitment to the poor may be sufficient. I then proceeded in the following section to examine Acts 8–28, showing that in these chapters, unexpectedly in the light of the gospel, Luke signals that the possession of material wealth is acceptable and not in the least an obstacle to salvation, and that any renunciation of personal belongings is unnecessary, even for the rich. In the subsequent section I turned to discussing the ways in which previous scholarship has sometimes attempted to dissolve the inconsistencies in Luke's treatment of possessions thus outlined. I argued that none of these is convincing and that we should therefore probably content ourselves with the notion that these discrepancies are real. I then proceeded in the subsequent section to offer an explanation for their existence. I did so by invoking and slightly refining the theory about Luke and Theophilus that I had sketched in chapter 1. Thus, in addition to what I had suggested there, I proposed that the few passages in Luke that deviate from its otherwise ascetic ethical outlook should be understood, in a manner of speaking, as "safety valves" in Luke's discourse, designed to keep Theophilus from rejecting the Christian faith in the event that he could not be swayed to adopt the ascetic lifestyle that most of the passages held out for him. In the last section, I turned to Acts 1–7. Since these chapters ascribe to the first congregation a community of goods and suggest that participation was mandatory for believers, one could have suspected that this part of Luke's work would offer a challenge to my theory that in Acts Luke had adapted his view of possessions to the preferences of Theophilus. Invoking and comparing it with one of Seneca's letters, however, I argued that it actually supports it. Thus, I argued that in the early chapters of Acts, Luke should be seen to have been trying to reinterpret the ascetic demands that he had advanced in the course of his gospel as applicable to all Christians of all times as in reality belonging only to a "golden age" that was now irretrievably lost, and that Luke should be seen to have done this because by so doing he enabled himself in the rest of his work to promote an ethical stance that was in tune with the wishes of Theophilus without seeming to contradict himself.

In chapter 4 I examined Luke's discourse on the family. I opened the chapter by clarifying the limits in our understanding of the institution of the ancient family and afterwards surveying the various approaches to the family that were taken by Christians in the early centuries of the church. This survey revealed a wide spectrum of positions. At one extreme, Clement of Alexandria ardently defended the family institution (while at the same time he strongly prohibited sex for reasons other than procreation). At the other, Marcion of Sinope (at least according to his detractors), by way of contrast, identified a full dissolution of all family ties as a soteriological requirement. After these studies I turned to examining Luke's stance on the family in Luke and Acts respectively. The analyses yielded results similar to those reached in chapter 3. Thus, on the one hand, they showed that in most of the passages in the gospel dealing with the family Luke assumed an ascetic position, very similar to the one taken by Marcion, with a few verses, however, offering a less rigorist message. On the other hand, they demonstrated that in Acts (except, to some extent, in the opening chapters of the book) he advanced a "pro-family" ideology, not dissimilar to the one advocated by Clement. After these explorations, I turned, in the final section, to discussing why Luke's stance on the family was characterized by these inconsistencies. I started out by noting that unlike the incongruities in his discourse on possessions, those in his outlook on the family appear to have gone largely unnoticed by biblical scholars. I then proceeded to examine whether my own theory about Luke and Theophilus might be able to serve as an explanatory model, and produced a positive answer.

The Unity of Luke and Acts Revisited

Let us now proceed to discuss how the readings that I have proposed may contribute to the debate about the unity of Luke and Acts. As noted at the outset of the study, Parsons and Pervo's *Rethinking the Unity of Luke and Acts* from 1993 distinguishes five different types of unity concerning Luke's writings: (1) authorial unity, (2) canonical unity, (3) generic unity, (4) narrative unity, and (5) theological unity. If we accept these distinctions, which I am happy to do, there can be no doubt that what I have focused on in this book relates to the fifth type of unity. It is therefore relevant to ask whether the readings that I have suggested confirm or refute the theological unity of Luke's writings.

When in chapter 1 I placed the present book in the context of this debate, I mentioned that "I would like to think of it as continuing in the line of those works" that have previously "challenged" the unity of Luke and Acts. That way of putting it was rather vague. But the vagueness was intentional. For although in this book I have emphasized the disparity between Luke's volumes, nevertheless I believe, and hope I have been able to show, that the question of the unity of these works is too complex to be answered with a simple "yes" or "no," even if we limit ourselves to discussing their theology.

In chapter 2 I focused on Luke's treatment of the topics of "Christianity and Rome," Christianity and novelty," and "Christianity and the Jews," and I argued there that Luke's attitude to these themes remained constant from the gospel to the Acts. Naturally, that by itself suggests unity between Luke and Acts. In chapters 3 and 4, however, I focused on Luke's treatment of the topics of material possessions and the family, and argued that his views of those subjects developed considerably from one work to the other. That, of course, points in the direction of *dis*unity. At the same time, however, to complicate matters further, I argued that Luke's description in the early chapters of Acts of the first congregation in Jerusalem was designed to leave his audience under the impression that his stance on possessions and the family had in fact remained unaltered throughout his work. Whether that points in the direction of unity or disunity must depend on whether we ask about how, at the time of the composition of the Acts, Luke *wanted* his readers to perceive his books or how he *feared* that they might perceive them.

Hence to conclude: if this book has contributed anything to the debate about the unity of Luke's writings it has done so not by settling it, or even attempting to do so, but by adding further complexity to it. It has shown that unity exists in some areas of the theology of these works, but not in others; and it has shown that when writing the Acts of the

Apostles, Luke seems to have wanted his audience to think of his works as theologically consistent, but also that he appears at that time to have been aware that they could be interpreted in a different fashion.

Bibliography

Alexander, L. C. A. “Reading Luke-Acts from Back to Front.” In *The Unity of Luke-Acts*, edited by J. Verheyden, 419–46. BETL 142. Leuven: Leuven University Press, 1999.

———. *The Preface to Luke's Gospel: Literary Convention and Social Context in Lk. 1.1–4 and Acts 1.1*. SNTSMS 78. Cambridge: Cambridge University Press, 1993.

———. “What If Luke Had Never Met Theophilus?” *BibInt* 8, no. 1 (2000): 161–70.

Alföldy, G. “Eine Bauinschrift aus dem Colosseum.” *ZPE* 109 (1994): 195–226.

Balch, D. L. “The Areopagus Speech: An Appeal to the Stoic Historian Posidonius against Later Stoics and the Epicureans.” In *Greeks, Romans, and Christians (FS Abraham Malherbe)*, edited by D. L. Balch, A. J. Malherbe, E. Ferguson, and W. A. Meeks, 52–79. Minneapolis, MN: Fortress Press, 1990.

Barclay, J. M. G. “The Family as Bearer of Religion in Judaism and Early Christianity.” In *Constructing Early Christian Families: Family as Social Reality and Metaphor*, edited by H. Moxnes, 66–80. London; New York, N.Y.: Routledge, 1997.

Barrett, C. K. *A Critical and Exegetical Commentary on the Acts of the Apostles. Vol. 2: Introduction and Commentary on Acts XV–XXVIII*. ICC 34. Edinburgh: T. & T. Clark, 1998.

———. *Luke the Historian in Recent Study*. London: Epworth, 1961.

———. “The Third Gospel as a Preface to Acts? Some Reflections.” In *The Four Gospels 1992 (FS Frans Neirynck). Vol. 2*, edited by F. van Segbroeck, C. M. Tuckett, G. van Belle, and J. Verheyden, 1451–66. BETL 100. Leuven: Leuven University Press, 1992.

Barton, S. C. *Discipleship and Family Ties in Mark and Matthew*. SNTSMS 80. Cambridge: Cambridge University Press, 1994.

Bauckham, R. "The Rich Man and Lazarus: The Parable and the Parallels." *NTS* 37, no. 2 (1991): 225–46.

Baugh, S. M. "Phraseology and the Reliability of Acts." *NTS* 36, no. 2 (1990): 290–4.

Bennett, J. *Trajan:* Optimus Princeps*: A Life and Times*. Bloomington, IN: Indiana University Press, 1997.

Bird, M. F. "The Unity of Luke-Acts in Recent Discussion." *JSNT* 29, no. 4 (2007): 425–48.

Black, M. *The Book of Enoch, Or, I Enoch: A New English Edition. With Commentary and Textual Notes*. SVTP 7. Leiden: Brill, 1985.

Blomberg, C. "The Law in Luke-Acts." *JSNT* 22 (1984): 53–80.

Bock, D. L. *Proclamation from Prophecy and Pattern: Lucan Old Testament Christology*. JSOTsup 12. Sheffield: JSOT Press, 1987.

Bonz, M. P. "Luke's Revision of Paul's Reflection in Romans 9–11." In *Early Christian Voices: In Texts, Traditions, and Symbols (FS François Bovon)*, edited by D. H. Warren, A. G. Brock, and D. W. Pao, 143–51. Biblical Interpretation Series 66. Boston, MS: Brill, 2003.

Bovon, F. *Das Evangelium nach Lukas 4, Lk 19,28–24,53*. EKK 3.4. Düsseldorf; Neukirchen-Vluyn: Patmos Verlag; Neukirchener Verlag, 2009.

———. *Lk. 1: A Commentary on the Gospel of Lk. 1:1–9:50*. Hermeneia. Minneapolis, MN: Fortress Press, 2002.

———. *Lk. 2: A Commentary on the Gospel of Lk. 9:51–19:27*. Hermeneia. Minneapolis, MN: Fortress Press, 2013.

Bradley, K. R. *Discovering the Roman Family: Studies in Roman Social History*. New York, N.Y.: Oxford University Press, 1991.

Brawley, R. L. *Luke-Acts and the Jews: Conflict, Apology, and Conciliation*. SBLMS 33. Atlanta, GA: Scholars Press, 1987.

Brown, P. *The Body and Society: Men, Women, and Sexual Renunciation in Early Christianity*. Lectures on the History of Religions 13. New York: Columbia University Press, 1988.

Burrus, V. *Chastity as Autonomy: Women in the Stories of the Apocryphal Acts*. Studies in Women and Religion 13. Lewiston, N.Y.: E. Mellen Press, 1987.

Cadbury, H. J. "Commentary on the Preface of Luke." In *The Beginnings of Christianity. Part I: The Acts of the Apostles. Vol. II*, edited by F. Jackson and K. Lake, 489–510. London: MacMillan, 1922.

———. "Some Foibles of New Testament Scholarship." *JBR* 26 (1958): 215–16.

———. *The Making of Luke-Acts*. 2nd ed. London: SPCK, 1958.

———. "The Purpose Expressed in Luke's Preface." *Expositor* 21 (1921): 431–41.

Capper, B. J. "Holy Community of Life and Property amongst the Poor: A Response to Steve Walton." *EvQ* 80, no. 2 (2008): 113–27.

———. "Reciprocity and the Ethics of Acts." In *Witness to the Gospel: The Theology of Acts*, edited by I. H. Marshall and D. Peterson, 499–518. Grand Rapids, MI: Eerdmans, 1998.

Cassidy, R. J. *Jesus, Politics and Society: A Study of Luke's Gospel*. Maryknoll, N.Y.: Orbis Books, 1978.

———. *Society and Politics in the Acts of the Apostles*. Maryknoll, N.Y.: Orbis Books, 1987.

Castelli, E. "Virginity and Its Meaning for Women's Sexuality in Early Christianity." *JFSR* 2, no. 1 (1986): 61–88.

Champlin, E. *Final Judgments: Duty and Emotion in Roman Wills, 200 B.C. – A.D. 250*. Berkeley, CA: California University Press, 1991.

Clark, A. C. *The Acts of the Apostles: A Critical Edition. With Introduction and Notes on Selected Passages*. Oxford: Clarendon, 1933.

Clark, E. A. "Antifamilial Tendencies in Ancient Christianity." *Journal of the History of Sexuality* 5, no. 3 (1995): 356–80.

———. *Reading Renunciation: Asceticism and Scripture in Early Christianity*. Princeton, N.J.: Princeton University Press, 1999.

Cohen, S. J. D. *The Beginnings of Jewishness: Boundaries, Varieties, Uncertainties*. Hellenistic Culture and Society 31. Berkeley, CA: University of California Press, 1999.

Co, M. A. "The Major Summarities in Acts: Acts 2,42–47; 4,32–35; 5,12–16." *ETL* 68 (1992): 49–85.

Conzelmann, H. *Acts of the Apostles: A Commentary on the Acts of the Apostles*. Hermeneia. Philadelphia: Fortress Press, 1987.

———. *The Theology of St. Luke.* New York, N.Y.: Harper, 1960.

Cooper, K. "The Household as a Venue for Religious Conversion: The Case of Christianity." In *A Companion to Families in the Greek and Roman Worlds,* edited by B. Rawson, 183–97. Blackwell Companions to the Ancient World: Literature and Culture. Chichester; Malden, MA: Wiley-Blackwell, 2010.

Countryman, L. W. *The Rich Christian in the Church of the Early Empire: Contradictions and Accommodations.* Texts and Studies in Religion 7. New York, N.Y.: E. Mellen Press, 1980.

D'Angelo, M. R. "'Knowing How to Preside over His Own Household': Imperial Masculinity and Christian Asceticism in the Pastorals, Hermas, and Luke-Acts." *Semeia* 45 (2003): 265–95.

———. "The ANHP Question in Luke-Acts: Imperial Masculinity and the Deployment of Women in the Early Second Century." In *A Feminist Companion to Luke,* edited by A. J. Levine, 44–69. London: Sheffield Academic Press, 2002.

———. "Women in Luke-Acts: A Redactional View." *JBL* 109, no. 3 (1990): 441–61.

Dawsey, J. "The Literary Unity of Luke-Acts: Questions of Style: A Task for Literary Critics." *NTS* 35, no. 1 (1989): 48–66.

Degenhardt, H.-J. *Lukas, Evangelist der Armen: Besitz und Besitzverzicht in den lukanischen Schriften: Eine traditions- und redaktionsgeschichtliche Untersuchung.* Stuttgart: Verlag Kath. Bibelwerk, 1965.

Dibelius, M. *Studies in the Acts of the Apostles.* New York, N.Y.: Charles Scribner's Sons, 1956.

Diderichsen, B. K. *Den markianske skilsmisseperikope: Dens genesis og historiske placering.* Copenhagen: Gyldendal, 1962.

Dixon, S. "Sex and the Married Woman in Ancient Rome." In *Early Christian Families in Context: An Interdisciplinary Dialogue,* edited by D. L. Balch and C. Osiek, 111–29. Religion, Marriage, and Family Series. Grand Rapids, MI: Eerdmans, 2003.

———. *The Roman Family.* Ancient Society and History. Baltimore: Johns Hopkins University Press, 1992.

———. "The Sentimental Ideal of the Roman Family." In *Marriage, Divorce, and Children in Ancient Rome,* edited by B. Rawson, 99–113. Oxford: Clarendon, 1991.

Dunn, J. D. G. *The Acts of the Apostles*. Epworth Commentaries. Valley Forge, PN: Trinity Press International, 1996.

Edwards, C. *The Politics of Immorality in Ancient Rome*. Cambridge; New York, N.Y.: Cambridge University Press, 1993.

Elliott, J. H. "Temple versus Household in Luke-Acts: A Contrast in Social Institutions." In *The Social World of Luke-Acts: Models for Interpretation*, edited by J. H. Neyrey, 211–40. Peabody, MS: Hendrickson Publishers, 1991.

Esler, Ph. F. *Community and Gospel in Luke-Acts: The Social and Political Motivations of Lucan Theology*. SNTSMS 57. Cambridge: Cambridge University Press, 1987.

Evans, C. A. "Prophecy and Polemic: Jews in Luke's Scriptural Polemic." In *Luke and Scripture: The Function of Sacred Tradition in Luke-Acts*, edited by C. A. Evans and J. A. Sanders, 171–211. Minneapolis, MN: Fortress Press, 1993.

Evans, C. F. *Saint Luke*. TPINTC. London; Philadelphia: SCM Press, 1990.

Feldman, L. H. *Jew and Gentile in the Ancient World: Attitudes and Interactions from Alexander to Justinian*. Princeton, N.J.: Princeton University Press, 1993.

Fitzmyer, J. A. *The Acts of the Apostles: A New Translation with Introduction and Commentary*. AB 31. New Haven, CN; London: Yale University Press, 1998.

———. *The Gospel According to Luke (I–IX): Introduction, Translation, and Notes*. AB 28. Garden City, N.Y.: Doubleday, 1981.

———. *The Gospel According to Luke (X–XXIV): Introduction, Translation, and Notes*. AB 28A. Garden City, N.Y.: Doubleday, 1983.

Fusco, V. "Luke-Acts and the Future of Israel." *NovT* 38, no. 1 (1996): 1–17.

Gaca, K. L. *The Making of Fornication: Eros, Ethics, and Political Reform in Greek Philosophy and Early Christianity*. Hellenistic Culture and Society 40. Berkeley, CA: University of California Press, 2003.

Gager, J. *The Origins of Anti-Semitism*. New York, N.Y.: Oxford University Press, 1983.

Gaston, L. "Anti-Judaism and the Passion Narrative in Luke and Acts." In *Anti-Judaism in Early Christianity. Vol. 1: Paul and the Gospels*, edited by P. Richardson and D. Granskou, 127–53. Studies in Christianity and Judaism 2. Waterloo, ON: Wilfrid Laurier University Press, 1986.

Gold, B. K. *Literary Patronage in Greece and Rome*. Chapel Hill, N.C.; London: University of North Carolina Press, 1987.

González, J. L. *Faith and Wealth: A History of Early Christian Ideas on the Origin, Significance, and Use of Money*. San Francisco, CA: Harper & Row, 1990.

Goodacre, M. S. *The Case Against Q: Studies in Markan Priority and the Synoptic Problem*. Harrisburg, PA: Trinity Press International, 2002.

Goodman, M. "The *Fiscus Iudaicus* and Gentile Attitudes to Judaism in Flavian Rome." In *Flavius Josephus and Flavian Rome*, edited by J. Edmondson, S. Mason, and J. Rives, 167–78. Oxford: Oxford University Press, 2005.

Goodspeed, E. J. "Some Greek Notes: Was Theophilus Luke's Publisher." *JBL* 73, no. 2 (1954): 84–92.

Gradl, H.-G. *Zwischen Arm und Reich: Das lukanische Doppelwerk in leserorientierter und textpragmatischer Perspektive*. FB 107. Würzburg: Echter, 2005.

Green, J. B. "Good News to Whom? Jesus and the 'Poor' in the Gospel of Luke." In *Jesus of Nazareth: Lord and Christ. Essays on the Historical Jesus and New Testament Christology*, edited by J. B. Green and M. Turner, 59–74. Grand Rapids, MI: Eerdmans, 1994.

———. *The Gospel of Luke*. NICNT. Grand Rapids, MI: Eerdmans, 1997.

Gregory, A. F. *The Reception of Luke and Acts in the Period before Irenaeus: Looking for Luke in the Second Century*. WUNT 2.169. Tübingen: Mohr Siebeck, 2003.

Gregory, A. F., and C. K. Rowe, eds. *Rethinking the Unity and Reception of Luke and Acts*. Columbia, S.C.: University of South Carolina Press, 2010.

Haenchen, E. "Judentum und Christentum in der Apostelgeschichte." *ZNW* 54 (1963): 155–87.

———. *The Acts of the Apostle: A Commentary*. Philadelphia, PA: Westminster, 1971.

———. "The Book of Acts as Source Material for the History of Early Christianity." In *Studies in Luke-Acts (FS Paul Schubert)*, edited by L. E. Keck and J. L. Martyn, 258–78. London: SPCK, 1968.

Hallbäck, G. *Apostlenes Gerninger fortolket*. Det Danske Bibelselskabs kommentarserie. Copenhagen: Det Danske Bibelselskab, 1993.

Hamm, D. "Lk. 19:8 Once Again: Does Zacchaeus Defend or Resolve?" *JBL* 107, no. 3 (1988): 431–37.

Harper, K. *From Shame to Sin: The Christian Transformation of Sexual Morality in Late Antiquity*. Revealing Antiquity 20. Cambridge, MA: Harvard University Press, 2013.

Hays, C. M. *Luke's Wealth Ethics: A Study in Their Coherence and Character*. WUNT 2.275. Tübingen: Mohr Siebeck, 2010.

Heil, C., and T. Klampfl. "Theophilos (Lk 1,3; Apg 1,1)." In *"Licht zur Erleuchtung der Heiden und Herrlichkeit für dein Volk Israels": Studien zum lukanischen Doppelwerk (FS Josef Zmijewski)*, edited by C. G. Müller, 7–28. BBB 151. Hamburg, 2005.

Heumann, C. A. "Dissertatio de Theophilo cui Lucas historiam sacram inscripsit," 1720. Chassis IV. Bibliotheca Historico-Philologico-Theologica.

Heusler, E. *Kapitalprozesse im lukanischen Doppelwerk*. NTAbh Neue Folge 38. Münster: Aschendorff, 2000.

Horn, F. W. *Glaube und Handeln in der Theologie des Lukas*. GTA 26. Göttingen: Vandenhoeck & Ruprecht, 1983.

Huebner, S. R. "Household Composition in the Ancient Mediterranean: What Do We Really Know?" In *A Companion to Families in the Greek and Roman Worlds*, edited by B. Rawson, 73–91. Blackwell Companions to the Ancient World: Literature and Culture. Chichester; Malden, MA: Wiley-Blackwell, 2011.

Hume, D. A. "'Sharing All Things in Common': Narrative, Alienation, and the Friendship Ethos in Acts 2:41–47 and 4:32–35." In *Law and Narrative in the Bible and in Neighbouring Ancient Cultures*, edited by K.-P. Adam, F. Avemarie, and D. Felsch, 327–47. FAT 2.54. Tübingen: Mohr Siebeck, 2012.

Hunter, D. G. *Marriage, Celibacy, and Heresy in Ancient Christianity: The Jovinianist Controversy*. Oxford Early Christian Studies. Oxford: Oxford University Press, 2007.

———. "'On the Sin of Adam and Eve': A Little-Known Defense of Marriage and Childbearing by Ambrosiaster." *HTR* 82, no. 3 (1989): 283–99.

Ireland, D. J. *Stewardship and the Kingdom of God: An Historical, Exegetical, and Contextual Study of the Parable of the Unjust Steward in Lk. 16:1–13*. SNT 70. Leiden: Brill, 1992.

Jervell, J. *Die Apostelgeschichte*. KEK 3. Göttingen: Vandenhoeck & Ruprecht, 1998.

Johnson, L. T. *The Acts of the Apostles*. SP 5. Collegeville, MI: Liturgical Press, 1992.

———. *The Gospel of Luke*. SP 3. Collegeville, MI: Liturgical Press, 1991.

———. *The Literary Function of Possessions in Luke-Acts*. SBLDS 39. Missoula, MT: Scholars Press, 1977.

Karris, R. J. "Rich and Poor: The Lukan Sitz-Im-Leben." In *Perspectives on Luke-Acts*, edited by C. H. Talbert, 112–25. SSS 5. Danville, VA: Assoc. of Baptist Professors of Religion, 1978.

Kim, K.-J. *Stewardship and Almsgiving in Luke's Theology*. JSNTsup 155. Sheffield: JSOT Press, 1998.

Klauck, H.-J. "Die Armut der Jünger in der Sicht des Lukas." In *Gemeinde, Amt, Sakrament: Neutestamentliche Perspektiven*, 160–94. Würzburg: Echter, 1989.

Kloppenborg, J. S. "The Dishonoured Master (Lk. 16:1–8a)." *Bib.* 70, no. 4 (1989): 474–95.

Köhler, W.-D. *Die Rezeption des Matthäusevangeliums in der Zeit vor Irenäus*. WUNT 2.24. Tübingen: Mohr, 1987.

Langlands, R. *Sexual Morality in Ancient Rome*. Cambridge: Cambridge University Press, 2006.

Laurence, R. "Introduction: From *Oikos* to *Familia*: Looking Forward." In *Families in the Greco-Roman World*, edited by R. Laurence and A. Strömberg, 1–9. The Family in Antiquity. London; New York, N.Y.: Continuum, 2012.

Légasse, S. *L'appel du riche (Marc 10:17–31 et parallèles): Contribution à l'étude des fondements scripturaires de l'état religieux*. Paris: Beauchesne, 1966.

Lehtipuu, O. "The Rich, the Poor, and the Promise of an Eschatological Reward in the Gospel of Luke." In *Other Worlds and Their Relation to This World*, edited by T. Nicklas, J. Verheyden, and M. M. Eynikel, 229–46. Supplement to the Journal for the Study of Judaism 143. Leiden; Boston, MS: Brill, 2010.

Loader, W. R. G. *The New Testament on Sexuality*. Attitudes towards Sexuality in Judaism and Christianity in the Hellenistic Greco-Roman Era. Grand Rapids, MI: Eerdmans, 2012.

Lygre, J. G. "Of What Charges? (Lk. 16:1–2)." *BTB* 32, no. 1 (2002): 21–28.

MacMullen, R. *Enemies of the Roman Order: Treason, Unrest, and Alienation in the Empire*. American Council of Learned Societies. Cambridge, MA: Harvard University Press, 1966.

Maddox, R. *The Purpose of Luke-Acts*. FRLANT 126. Edinburgh: T. & T. Clark, 1982.

Manson, T. W. *The Sayings of Jesus, as Recorded in the Gospels According to St. Matthew and St. Luke*. London: SCM Press, 1949.

Marguerat, D. *The First Christian Historian: Writing the "Acts of the Apostles."* SNTSMS 121. Cambridge: Cambridge University Press, 2002.

Marshall, I. H. "Acts and the 'Former Treatise.'" In *The Book of Acts in Its First Century Setting. Vol. 1: Ancient Literary Setting*, edited by B. W. Winter and A. D. Clarke, 163–82. Grand Rapids, MI: Eerdmans, 1993.

———. *The Acts of the Apostles: An Introduction and Commentary*. TNTC. Leicester; Grand Rapids, MI: Inter-Varsity; Eerdmans, 1980.

———. *The Gospel of Luke: A Commentary on the Greek Text*. NIGTC. Exeter: Paternoster, 1978.

Martin, D. B. "Paul without Passion: On Paul's Rejection of Desire in Sex and Marriage." In *Constructing Early Christian Families: Family as Social Reality and Metaphor*, edited by H. Moxnes, 201–15. London; New York, N.Y.: Routledge, 1997.

———. "The Construction of the Ancient Family: Methodological Considerations." *JRS* 86 (1996): 40–60.

Mason, S. *Josephus and the New Testament*. 2nd ed. Peabody, MS: Hendrickson Publishers, 2003.

———. *Josephus, Judea, and Christian Origins: Methods and Categories*. Peabody, MS: Hendrickson Publishers, 2009.

Matera, F. J. *New Testament Christology*. Louisville, KY: Westminster John Knox Press, 1999.

Matson, D. L. *Household Conversion Narratives in Acts: Pattern and Interpretation*. JSNTsup 123. Sheffield: Sheffield Academic Press, 1996.

McGinn, T. A. J. *Prostitution, Sexuality, and the Law in Ancient Rome*. New York, N.Y.: Oxford University Press, 1998.

Mealand, D. "Community of Goods and Utopian Allusions in Acts II–IV." *JTS* 28 (1977): 96–9.

Metzger, J. A. *Consumption and Wealth in Luke's Travel Narrative*. Biblical Interpretation Series 88. Leiden; Boston, MS: Brill, 2007.

Millar, F. "Last Year in Jerusalem: Monuments of War in Rome 1." In *Flavius Josephus and Flavian Rome*, edited by J. Edmondson, S. Mason, and J. Rives, 101–30. Oxford: Oxford University Press, 2005.

Mineshige, K. *Besitzverzicht und Almosengeben: Wesen und Forderung des lukanischen Vermögensethos*. WUNT 2.163. Tübingen: Mohr Siebeck, 2003.

Mitchell, A. C. "The Social Function of Friendship in Acts 2:44–47 and 4:32–37." *JBL* 111, no. 2 (1992): 255–72.

———. "Zacchaeus Revisited: Lk. 19,8 as a Defense." *Bib.* 71 (1990): 153–76.

Moessner, D. P. "Paul in Acts: Preacher of Eschatological Repentance to Israel." *NTS* 34, no. 1 (1988): 96–104.

Moore, S. D. "Are the Gospels Unified Narratives?" In *Society of Biblical Literature 1987 Seminar Papers*, edited by K. H. Richards, 443–58. SBLSP 26. Atlanta, GA: Scholars Press, 1987.

Moss, C. R. *The Myth of Persecution: How Early Christians Invented a Story of Martyrdom*. New York, N.Y.: HarperOne, 2013.

Moxnes, H. *The Economy of the Kingdom: Social Conflict and Economic Relations in Luke's Gospel*. Philadelphia, PA: Fortress Press, 1988.

———. "What Is Family? Problems in Constructing Early Christian Families." In *Constructing Early Christian Families: Family as Social Reality and Metaphor*, edited by H. Moxnes, 13–41. London; New York, N.Y.: Routledge, 1997.

Neyrey, J. H. "Acts 17, Epicureans, and Theodicy: A Study in Stereotypes." In *Greeks, Romans, and Christians (FS Abraham Malherbe)*, edited by D. L. Balch, A. J. Malherbe, E. Ferguson, and W. A. Meeks, 118–34. Minneapolis, MN: Fortress Press, 1990.

———. "The Symbolic Universe of Luke-Acts." In *The Social World of Luke-Acts: Models for Interpretation*, edited by J. H. Neyrey, 271–304. Peabody, MS: Hendrickson Publishers, 1991.

Nippel, W. *Public Order in Ancient Rome*. Key Themes in Ancient History. Cambridge; New York, N.Y.: Cambridge University Press, 1995.

Osiek, C. *Shepherd of Hermas: A Commentary*. Hermeneia. Minneapolis, MN: Fortress Press, 1999.

Osiek, C., and D. L. Balch. *Families in the New Testament World: Households and House Churches*. The Family, Religion, and Culture. Louisville, KY: Westminster John Knox Press, 1997.

Osiek, C., M. Y. MacDonald, and J. H. Tulloch. *A Woman's Place: House Churches in Earliest Christianity*. Minneapolis, MN: Fortress Press, 2006.

O'Toole, R. F. *The Unity of Luke's Theology: An Analysis of Luke-Acts*. GNS 9. Wilmington, DE: M. Glazier, 1984.

Parsons, M. C. "'Short in Stature': Luke's Physical Description of Zacchaeus." *NTS* 47, no. 1 (2001): 50–57.

Parsons, M. C., and R. I. Pervo. *Rethinking the Unity of Luke and Acts*. Minneapolis, MN: Fortress Press, 1993.

Pervo, R. I. *Acts: A Commentary*. Hermeneia. Minneapolis, MN: Fortress Press, 2009.

———. *Dating Acts: Between the Evangelists and the Apologists*. Santa Rosa, CA: Polebridge Press, 2006.

Pesch, R. *Die Apostelgeschichte*. EKK 5. Zürich: Benziger, 1986.

Petracca, V. *Gott oder das Geld: Die Besitzethik des Lukas*. Texte und Arbeiten zum neutestamentlichen Zeitalter 39. Tübingen: Francke, 2003.

Phillips, T. E. *Reading Issues of Wealth and Poverty in Luke-Acts*. Studies in Bible and Early Christianity 48. Lewiston, N.Y.: E. Mellen Press, 2001.

Pilhofer, P. *Presbyteron kreitton: Der Altersbeweis der jüdischen und christlichen Apologeten und seine Vorgeschichte*. WUNT 2.39. Tübingen: Mohr Siebeck, 1990.

Räisänen, H. "The Redemption of Israel: A Salvation-Historical Problem in Luke-Acts." In *Luke-Acts: Scandinavian Perspectives*, edited by P. Luomanen, 94–114. Publications of the Finnish Exegetical Society 54. Göttingen: Vandenhoeck & Ruprecht, 1991.

Ravens, D. A. S. "Zacchaeus: The Final Part of a Lucan Triptych?" *JSNT* 41 (1991): 19–32.

Regul, J. *Die antimarcionitischen Evangelienprologe*. Vetus Latina. Die Reste der altlateinischen Bibel. Aus der Geschichte der lateinischen Bibel 6. Freiburg: Herder, 1969.

Reydams-Schils, G. *The Roman Stoics: Self, Responsibility, and Affection*. Chicago, IL: University of Chicago Press, 2005.

Roose, H. "Umkehr und Ausgleich bei Lukas: Die Gleichnisse vom verlorenen Sohn (Lk 15.11–32) und vom reichen Mann und armen Lazarus (Lk 16.19–31) als Schwestergeschichten." *NTS* 56, no. 1 (2010): 1–21.

Rowe, C. K. "History, Hermeneutics, and the Unity of Luke-Acts." *JSNT* 28, no. 2 (2005): 131–57.

———. "Literary Unity and Reception History: Reading Luke-Acts as Luke and Acts." *JSNT* 29, no. 4 (2007): 449–57.

———. "The Grammar of Life: The Areopagus Speech and Pagan Tradition." *NTS* 57, no. 1 (2011): 31–50.

———. *World Upside Down: Reading Acts in the Graeco-Roman Age*. Oxford; New York, N.Y.: Oxford University Press, 2009.

Russell, H. G. "Which Was Written First, Luke or Acts?" *HTR* 48, no. 3 (1955): 167–74.

Saller, R. P. "'*Familia, Domus*,' and the Roman Conception of the Family." *Phoenix* 38, no. 4 (1984): 336–55.

Saller, R. P., and B. D. Shaw. "Tombstones and Roman Family Relations in the Principate: Civilians, Soldiers and Slaves." *JRS* 74 (1984): 124–56.

Sanders, J. T. "The Jewish People in Luke-Acts." In *Luke-Acts and the Jewish People: Eight Perspectives*, edited by J. B. Tyson, 51–75. Minneapolis, MN: Augsburg, 1988.

———. *The Jews in Luke-Acts*. London: SCM Press, 1987.

Schellenberg, R. S. "Which Master? Whose Steward? Metalepsis and Lordship in the Parable of the Prudent Steward (Lk. 16.1–13)." *JSNT* 30, no. 3 (2008): 263–88.

Schmid, J. *Das Evangelium nach Matthäus*. RNT 1. Regensburg: Friedrich Pustet, 1959.

Schmidt, T. E. *Hostility to Wealth in the Synoptic Gospels*. JSNTsup 15. Sheffield: JSOT Press, 1987.

Schneider, G. *Verleugnung, Verspottung und Verhör Jesu nach Lukas 22, 54–71: Studien zur lukanischen Darstellung der Passion.* SANT 22. Munich: Kösel-Verlag, 1969.

Schottroff, L., and W. Stegemann. *Jesus von Nazareth: Hoffnung der Armen.* Stuttgart: W. Kohlhammer, 1990.

Seccombe, D. P. *Possessions and the Poor in Luke-Acts.* SNTSU, B 6. Linz: A. Fuchs, 1982.

Seim, T. K. *The Double Message: Patterns of Gender in Luke-Acts.* Studies of the New Testament and Its World. Edinburgh: T. & T. Clark, 1994.

Sterling, G. E. *Historiography and Self-Definition: Josephos, Luke-Acts and Apologetic Historiography.* SNT 64. New York, N.Y.: Brill, 1992.

———. "'Opening the Scriptures': The Legitimation of the Jewish Diaspora and the Early Christian Mission." In *Jesus and the Heritage of Israel: Luke's Narrative Claim upon Israel's Legacy,* edited by D. P. Moessner, 199–217. Luke the Interpreter of Israel. Vol. 1. Harrisburg, PA: Trinity Press, 1999.

Stivala, J. "The Christian After-Life of Seneca the Younger: The First Four Hundred Years." Ph.D., Australian National University, 2009.

Strauss, M. L. *The Davidic Messiah in Luke-Acts: Promise and Its Fulfillment in Lukan Christology.* JSNTsup 110. Sheffield: JSOT Press, 1995.

Tannehill, R. C. "Israel in Luke-Acts: A Tragic Story." *JBL* 104, no. 1 (1985): 69–85.

———. *The Narrative Unity of Luke-Acts: A Literary Interpretation. Vol. 1: The Gospel according to Luke.* Philadelphia, PA: Fortress Press, 1986.

———. *The Narrative Unity of Luke-Acts: A Literary Interpretation. Vol. 2: The Acts of the Apostles.* Minneapolis, MN: Fortress Press, 1994.

———. "The Story of Israel within Luke's Narrative." In *Jesus and the Heritage of Israel: Luke's Narrative Claim upon Israel's Legacy,* edited by D. P. Moessner, 325–39. Luke the Interpreter of Israel. Vol. 1. Harrisburg, PA: Trinity Press, 1999.

Taylor, J. "The Community of Goods among the First Christians and among the Essenes." In *Historical Perspectives: From the Hasmoneans to Bar Kokhba in Light of the Dead Sea Scrolls,* edited by D. M. Goodblatt, A. Pinnick, and D. R. Schwartz, 147–61. STDJ 37. Boston, MS.: Brill, 2001.

Theißen, G. *Soziologie der Jesusbewegung: Eine Beitrag zur Entstehungsgeschichte des Urchristentums.* Theologische Existenz Heute 194. Munich: Kaiser, 1977.

———. "Wanderradikalismus: Literatursoziologische Aspekte der Überlieferung von Worten Jesu im Urchristentum." *ZTK* 70 (1973): 245–71.

Thiessen, M. *Contesting Conversion: Genealogy, Circumcision, and Identity in Ancient Judaism and Christianity.* Oxford: Oxford University Press, 2011.

Tiede, D. L. *Prophecy and History in Luke-Acts.* Philadelphia, PA: Fortress Press, 1980.

Trebilco, P. *The Early Christians in Ephesus from Paul to Ignatius.* Grand Rapids, MI: Eerdmans, 2008.

Treggiari, S. *Roman Marriage:* Iusti Coniuges *from the Time of Cicero to the Time of Ulpian.* Oxford: Clarendon, 1991.

Troeltsch, E. *Die Soziallehren der christlichen Kirchen und Gruppen.* Tübingen: J.C.B. Mohr, 1923.

Tyson, J. B. *Images of Judaism in Luke-Acts.* Columbia, S.C.: University of South Carolina Press, 1992.

Verheyden, J., ed. *The Unity of Luke-Acts.* BETL 142. Leuven: Leuven University Press, 1999.

Wainwright, A. W. "Luke and the Restoration of the Kingdom to Israel." *ExpTim* 89 (78 1977): 76–9.

Walaskay, P. *"And So We Came to Rome": The Political Perspective of St. Luke.* SNTSMS 49. Cambridge: Cambridge University Press, 1983.

Walton, S. "Primitive Communism in Acts? Does Acts Present the Community of Goods (2:44–45; 4:32–35) as Mistaken?" *EvQ* 80, no. 2 (2008): 99–111.

Watson, F. *Gospel Writing: A Canonical Perspective.* Grand Rapids, MI: Eerdmans, 2013.

Weiss, J. *Über die Absicht und den literarischen Charakter der Apostelgeschichte.* Göttingen: Vandenhoeck & Ruprecht, 1897.

Williams, C. A. *Roman Homosexuality.* 2nd ed. Oxford; New York, N.Y.: Oxford University Press, 2010.

Wills, L. M. "The Depiction of the Jews in Acts." *JBL* 110, no. 4 (1991): 631–54.

Wilson, S. G. “Lukan Eschatology.” *NTS* 16, no. 4 (1970): 330–47.

———. *Luke and the Law*. SNTSMS 50. Cambridge: Cambridge University Press, 1983.

Winsbury, R. *The Roman Book: Books, Publishing and Performance in Classical Rome*. Classical Literature and Society. London: Duckworth, 2009.

Winter, P. *On the Trial of Jesus*. SJ 1. Berlin; New York, N.Y.: De Gruyter, 1974.

Witherington, B. *The Acts of the Apostles: A Socio-Rhetorical Commentary*. Grand Rapids, MI: Eerdmans, 1998.

Wolter, M. *Das Lukasevangelium*. HNT 5. Tübingen: Mohr Siebeck, 2008.

———. *Theologie und Ethos im frühen Christentum: Studien zu Jesus, Paulus und Lukas*. WUNT 236. Tübingen: Mohr Siebeck, 2009.

Zeller, E. *Die Apostelgeschichte nach ihrem Inhalt und Ursprung kritisch untersucht*. Stuttgart: Mäcken, 1854.

Zmijewski, J. *Die Eschatologiereden des Lukas-Evangeliums: Eine traditions- und redaktionsgeschichtliche Untersuchung zu Lk 21, 5–36 und Lk 17, 20–37*. Bonn: P. Hanstein, 1972.

Index